HOW TO MASTER YOUR INNER SUPERMAN:

A GUIDE FOR MALE SURVIVORS OF CHILDHOOD SEXUAL ABUSE USING SUPERMAN TO HELP CONQUER THE NEED FOR FACADES

By Kenneth Rogers, Jr.

Strategic Book Publishing and Rights Co.

Strategic Book Publishing and Rights Co., LLC
USA | Singapore
www.sbpra.net

For information about special discounts for bulk purchases, please contact Strategic Book Publishing and Rights Co., LLC. Special Sales, at bookorder@sbpra.net.

ISBN: 978-1-62212-211-0

BOOKS BY KENNETH ROGERS, JR.

Nonfiction

How to Kill Your Batman: A Guide for Male Survivors of Childhood Sexual Abuse Using Batman to Heal Hypervigilance

- NABE Pinnacle Achievement Book Award
- Reader's Favorite Book Award Five Star Review

Heroes, Villains and Healing: A Guide for Male Survivors of Childhood Sexual Abuse Using DC Superheroes and Villains

- Independent Press Award
- National Indie Book Award
- Beverly Hills Book Award
- NABE Pinnacle Achievement Book Award

Raped Black Male: A Memoir

Young Adult Fantasy

Chronicles of the Last Liturian Book One: The Diary of Oliver Lee

Chronicles of the Last Liturian Book Two: Love and Fear

Chronicles of the Last Liturian Book Three: Infinite Truths and Impossible Dreams

Science Fiction

Sequence

- Next Generation Indie Book Award
- NABE Pinnacle Achievement Book Award

Speculative Fiction

Thoughts in Italics

Writing in the Margins

TABLE OF CONTENTS

INTRODUCTION

"That's why I wear the costume. I learned years ago that if people knew about me, I'd have no peace. I'd be a freak, a curiosity. A monster even."

Clark Kent—*Superman: Secret Identity (2004)*

When I was a boy, Superman was (beyond a doubt) my favorite superhero. To me, the Man of Steel embodied the definition of what it meant to be a hero. Not only because he could fly, but also because he was my first exposure to comics after purchasing *The Death of Superman* (1992). As I grew older, I soon came to realize most of my favorite TV shows and movies involved the Man of Steel. Shows such as *Superman: The Animated Series*, *Lois and Clark: The New Adventures of Superman*, and *Smallville* were always a must-watch on Saturday mornings or Wednesday nights just before bed. Seeing either the emblazoned "S" on Superman's chest or the wire-rim glasses as Clark Kent pulled them from his face stirred an emotion that was undefinable but palpable. At the time there was no definitive answer to why he was my favorite superhero, besides the simple fact that he had laser vision and super strength. Even as an adult, I knew I loved Superman as a superhero and Clark Kent as a good man, but I did not know why. He was just Superman, the first and the best superhero of all time. However, after researching, writing, and reflecting on this guide and my own childhood sexual abuse, I was presented with an opportunity to finally find the words needed to articulate my love of the Big Blue Boy Scout.

Writing two self-help guides for male survivors, *How to Kill Your Batman*, and *How to Master Your Inner Superman*, were invaluable in helping me understand how to articulate the impact of childhood sexual abuse on male survivors; my role as a man, black male, role model, and public educator throughout my community; the impact of my words and actions as a father and husband on the development of my children and the well-being of my wife; and lessons in how to create inclusive material that has the ability to benefit all male survivors seeking to heal from the trauma of childhood sexual abuse. Writing each guide helped me understand myself and childhood sexual abuse, but also helped me better understand Batman and Superman as superheroes, fictional characters, and their ability to invoke powerful (and sometimes visceral) emotions in readers of all ages and genders.

For example, while researching, reading, and writing the self-help guide *How to Kill Your Batman,* there were times I had to take a break, because there were moments when I felt myself becoming more like Batman, but not in the cool way. Rather than punching bad guys and driving expensive cars, I became anxious, brooding, irritable, and constantly in want of being left alone. My moods and mental health took a turn for the worse. Following its publication, I became relieved that I no longer had to analyze, interpret, and explain how Batman could be used to overcome the need for hypervigilance. On the other hand, when beginning to read and research *How to Master Your Inner Superman,* there was an immediate difference in the effect stories involving Superman had on my mood and outlook on life. Rather than constantly planning for worst-case scenarios, I found myself filled with a sense of hope and optimism for the new day. The Superman story that I enjoyed reading the most and which seemed to embody these feelings was Kurt Busiek's *Superman: Secret Identity* (2004).

Superman: Secret Identity is and is not a Superman story. The main character's name is Clark Kent, but not *the* Clark Kent. He eventually becomes Superman, but not *the* Superman. While it may be the best Superman comic I have yet to read, my description of the plot would not do it justice. Beneath the surface of super abilities, heroes, and villains are invaluable lessons that reveal less about Superman and the facade he presents to the world, and more about what it means to live a life filled with happiness, mistakes, love, family, growing old, becoming wise, and the passing of legacies on to the next generation. Few comics have had the ability to induce such emotions and to make me cry, but this one did, and I highly recommend reading it in its entirety.

Long after the last page of *Superman: Secret Identity* was read and the comic was stored on the shelf, the messages and life lessons remained with me. Unlike epic graphic novels centered around Batman, such as *The Long Halloween* (1997), I did not find myself becoming paranoid and irritable after it came to an end. Instead, I developed the capacity to be more patient, express more hope, and realize I did not want to kill my Superman. Killing my Superman was too final. Too morbid. I needed my Superman to remain hopeful that the Man of Tomorrow could somehow help in evolving into a better man by eliminating the need to mask my emotions behind a facade of stoicism. I needed to conquer the facades of my Superman, not only for myself, but for my wife, my two daughters, and my students if I was to become a better husband, father, educator, and advocate for survivors of sexual abuse and assault. This guide is an attempt to live up to those obligations.

To help male survivors understand and recover from the trauma of childhood sexual abuse, this guide focuses on three forms of therapy that can help conquer the need to mask feelings and emotions with a facade: Dialectical Behavior Therapy, Internal Family Structure Therapy, and Cognitive Behavior Therapy. This guide also uses the three separate identities of Superman—Clark Kent, Superman, and Kal-El—to understand the facades male survivors portray to negate feelings of shame associated with the trauma of sexual abuse. While Superman comics are referenced as a means to heal the trauma of childhood sexual abuse, I highly recommend purchasing and reading each comic listed in the "Further Reading" section of this guide. It is the only way to give homage to the authors and artists and to fully appreciate the beauty of their words and images that come together to tell wonderful stories through the magic of comics.

Dialectical Behavior Therapy (DBT)

Dialectical Behavior Therapy (DBT) was developed in the 1980s on principles of Zen Buddhist philosophy. Dialectical refers to the synthesis of opposites and seeks to recognize that radical acceptance is necessary for change and growth, focusing on mindfulness, emotion regulation, distress tolerance, and interpersonal effectiveness. The theories of DBT are used in conjunction with Superman comics to help male survivors understand the need to associate (merge) different facades and to become open to exposing and feeling a full range of emotions.

Internal Family Systems (IFS) Therapy

Internal Family System (IFS) Therapy was developed by Dr. Richard Schwartz. It breaks the self into three parts: exiles, managers, and firefighters. The exile is a portion of the self that carries the burden of the trauma; the manager is a portion of the self that protects the survivor from vulnerability created after the sexual abuse; and the firefighter is a portion of the self that acts out to repress feelings of shame associated with the trauma. The goal of IFS is not to eliminate the **exile, manager,** and **firefighter,** but to develop the three relationships with the self to feel calm, confident, and in control. The theories of IFS are used in conjunction with the facades of Clark Kent, Superman, and Kal-El to help male survivors understand the function of their facade following sexual abuse.

Cognitive Behavior Therapy (CBT)

Cognitive Behavior Therapy (CBT) was originally developed by Dr. Aaron Beck and is one of the most effective forms of therapy used to combat **post-traumatic stress disorder (PTSD).** It uses the ability to express the traumatic event of the past through writing and dialogue in an attempt to combat the negative thoughts of the traumatic memory. CBT helps survivors change their automatic thoughts from negative beliefs to positive truths that are free of cognitive distortions. The theories of CBT are used in conjunction with Superman comics to help male survivors understand the healing process, begin the journey toward recovery, and eliminate feelings of shame.

What is a Facade?

Survivors of childhood sexual abuse tend to feel isolated and ostracized. This occurs because positive self-esteem and full development of the self, which is meant to occur during childhood and adolescence, is stripped away following the violation. To combat the sense of shame associated with childhood sexual abuse, some male survivors hide parts of their personalities considered to be weak or not acceptable by expectations of what it means to be a "real" man, creating a facade, or a false identity. These individuals rarely, if ever, let others witness their full range of emotions. On the surface, these male survivors may work, play, and behave as if everything is normal. However, beneath the surface of their facade, the trauma of being sexually abused as a child causes them to find it difficult letting friends, family, or loved ones see their pain, suffering, and confusion out of fear of being seen as a "lesser man." This need to present a facade to the world as a means of protection for themselves, friends, family, and loved ones can be seen in the same way Superman presents different facades to the world in an attempt to protect the people he cares about from discovering his true identity.

Clark Kent, Superman, and Kal-El

Superman is a fictional superhero created by writer Jerry Siegel and artist Joe Shuster. The two Cleveland-born storytellers were the first to imagine an alien rocket landing in the fields of Smallville, Kansas, carrying the cargo of a baby boy from the distant, destroyed planet of Krypton. Upon arrival, the boy is found and adopted by farmers Jonathan and Martha Kent. The married couple (unable to have children of their own) adopt the boy, name him Clark (Martha Kent's maiden name) and raise him on their family farm. To protect Clark, Jonathan and Martha hide the secret of his extraterrestrial origins from others (and Clark) by concealing the rocket in their cellar and by raising Clark as if he is no different from anyone else.

As a boy, Clark comes of age with a sense of normalcy. He has two loving parents, two close friends (Lana Lang and Pete Ross), and no special abilities. However, during adolescence, Clark develops superhuman abilities to run faster than a speeding locomotive, leap the family farmhouse in a single bound, stop the blades of a combine tractor with his bare hands without receiving a single scratch, and defy the laws of gravity with the ability to fly. Concerned for the safety of their son, Jonathan and Martha Kent reveal the truth of Clark's alien origin. Upon revealing the rocket, Clark learns (through the assistance of the holographic image of his birth parents, Jor-El and Lara) of his Kryptonian origins, the destruction of his home planet, and his Kryptonian name, Kal-El.

As an adult, Clark decides to use his super abilities to fight crime and to inspire hope throughout humanity. To remain connected to humanity, he assumes the alter ego of a mild-mannered reporter for the Metropolis newspaper, the *Daily Planet.* Throughout Clark's journey as a hero, he continues to learn of his Kryptonian heritage while attempting to remain loyal to humanity's morals and the parental teachings of truth, justice, and preservation of life at all costs.

Why Superman?

Although Superman is a superhero, he attempts to live a normal, human existence and hide his superhuman abilities by trying to fit in with others. Many male survivors of childhood sexual abuse also attempt to look and behave in a normal manner to the rest of world in an attempt to alleviate the sense of shame associated with their abuse.

These qualities make Clark Kent, Superman, and Kal-El ideal characters to assist in helping male survivors understand the effects of sexual trauma in reinforcing walls meant to protect themselves and survive. As a superhero, the different facades of Clark Kent, Superman, and Kal-El embody many of the traits of male survivors in the form of lowered self-esteem and self-sacrifice for the greater good.

Was I Sexually Abused?

As you begin to conquer your Superman, you, as a male survivor of childhood sexual abuse, may ask yourself, "Was I sexually abused as a child?" There is no easy way to answer this question. This is because admitting the answer would mean acknowledging your weakness as a child, the abuse you survived, and the healing journey you are beginning to take.

Before beginning to reflect on your past to answer this difficult question, take a moment to acknowledge that you are not alone. There are other survivors. Other males have experienced sexual trauma in their childhood and have grown stronger as adults after coming to terms with, and mourning the loss of, the childhood they were forced to endure. To determine if you were sexually abused as a child or teen, some questions you may ask yourself are:

- Was I raped or otherwise penetrated?
- Was I forced to penetrate someone else?
- Was I made to watch sexual acts either in person or on pornographic videos?
- Was I forced to perform oral sex?
- Was I made to pose naked for an adult's gratification?
- Was I made to fondle another male or female against my will?
- Was I forced to take part in ritualized abuse in which I was physically, psychologically, or sexually tortured?

These are not easy questions to answer. However, if you answered yes to any of these questions, you have come a long way. I commend you for surviving. I know the pain you endured was real and should not be minimized. As you begin to reflect on your sexual abuse and your approach to healing, you may feel lost, confused, and unable to interpret your role in the sexual abuse. This is normal. Take time to process these thoughts. Knowing you were abused, who abused you, and being able to tell your story is one of the first steps toward understanding your trauma. This is difficult but necessary. You may not be able to do it just yet. Take the time you need. If you feel anxious or in a panic at any time while reading this guide, put down the book for as long as you need. Rest, reflect, and return when you are ready.

Why Only Write for Male Survivors?

Beyond a doubt, *How to Conquer Your Inner Superman* can be used to help more than just male survivors of childhood sexual abuse. The analogies used to describe facade, mindfulness, and recovering from post-traumatic stress disorder (PTSD) can also be helpful for female survivors of sexual abuse and military veterans suffering from PTSD. No matter what the trauma may be, it has similar effects on the mind and body of any survivor. However, the stigmas applied to each form of trauma throughout our society make understanding the trauma and the road to recovery different for each survivor. It is for this reason I write for male survivors of childhood sexual abuse.

I am not a psychiatrist, therapist, or counselor for trauma or sexual abuse. I am a writer, secondary educator, father, husband, and male survivor of childhood sexual abuse. This means, for now, I am only comfortable writing about the trauma I know of and have experienced. It is a trauma I have suffered and continue to recover from. This book is an extension of my recovery. It is an attempt to help other male survivors while understanding the effects my sexual abuse has had throughout all aspects of my life. It is a refusal to remain silent while providing a voice for myself and other survivors who feel they must remain silent.

This book is written specifically for male survivors because male survivors of sexual abuse are often ignored and made to believe they do not exist. Writing specifically for male survivors helps to foster a safe community for them. Creating this community allows awareness of male survivors to be recognized throughout society.

To ensure healing for male survivors, the community must take an active role in acknowledging the male survivor's abuse—that it did occur. This cannot be done in the shadows. While the "Me Too" movement has begun to shed light on the sexual assault, abuse, and rape of women, much more still has to be done to provide the needed support for female survivors. Meanwhile, there is even less support available for male survivors. Without the same light being shown on the sexual abuse of boys and men, male survivors continue to feel shame, humiliation, and guilt for an abuse they had no control over. Without any recognition and restitution by the community in which we live, male survivors will never be given the opportunity to heal.

In their article "Rape Trauma Syndrome," Burgess and Holmstrom found that women who made the best recoveries were those who had become advocates of the antirape movement, so why shouldn't the same be assumed to be true for male survivors? Unfortunately, male survivors feel as if they must continue to hide and that they are the only individuals who have suffered this trauma, forcing them to feel weak and victimized. Soldiers and survivors of war have living monuments where they can express their grief, loss, and trauma, while survivors of sexual assault and abuse suffer without the possibility of a living anchor to tether their trauma. Judith Herman explains that, "in refusing to hide or be silenced, in insisting that rape is a pubic matter, and in demanding social change, survivors create their own living monument." This book, and others like it, are my attempt to not be silenced and to create a living anchor for other male survivors like myself.

PART ONE:
THE CLARK KENT FACADE

"People have to know that there's another way, Lois. They have to hear a voice of compassion and faith instead of spite and anger. They have to see that someone believes in humanity strongly enough—"

"To die for them?"

Clark Kent & **Lois Lane**—*Superman*, "What's So Funny About Truth, Justice, and the American Way?" (2001)

In Alan Moore's 1985 classic *The Jungle Line*, Superman becomes infected by the ancient Kryptonian fungus bloodmorel. The ancient fungus creates a disease in the blood of the superhero, causing hallucinations and eventual death as the Kryptonian host exerts himself in an attempt to survive. Once exposed to the fungus, Clark's powers as Superman begin to waver without warning or explanation, creating moments of shock following the hero's first paper cut, and entering a supply closet in which two coworkers are "alone" in the dark.

As the fungus takes root, Clark experiences a nightmare in which the separate personalities of Superman and Clark Kent argue with one another. In the hallucination, Superman's costume (absent of a body) says to an empty two-button suit and glasses, "Kal, you're dying. It isn't right that you should end up like this. You're a legend! You've got to fight it, Kal." The mild-mannered suit responds, "With respect, Superman, I, uh, don't agree. I mean, without your powers you aren't, uh, anybody special. Death comes to everyone in the end. You're no exception. Lie back and accept it." Clark wakes up in anger and fear, screaming for the separate personalities to shut up.

Unsure of how to wage war against the growing infection pulsating throughout his body, Superman investigates the fungus in an attempt to create an antidote. However, he soon reaches the conclusion that without the consistency of his powers there is nothing he can do to reverse the viral effects. Rather than seek help from Batman, Flash, or Wonder Woman, Clark chooses to die alone.

While clutching the rock that contains the Kryptonian fungus, Clark buys a used car and drives south. With a haggard beard, Clark wavers in and out of consciousness, hallucinates, runs off the road, and crashes. Emerging from the wreckage in a ball of flames and holding the Kryptonian spore, Clark falls to the ground and enters a hallucination in which he is battling for his life in the Scarlet Jungle of Krypton.

Alone and knocking on death's door, the antihero Swamp Thing happens upon the fallen superhero. Beneath Clark's incinerated shirt and jacket he sees the blue, red, and yellow costume and knows the person before him is Superman. Swamp Thing attempts to help the fallen hero, but, believing he is being attacked, Superman burns a whole in the chest of the swamp monster with his heat vision and becomes filled with so much rage that he destroys the forest around him. Eventually, Swamp Thing convinces Superman to realize that if he does not control his rage and calm his mind, he will die from exhaustion. With Swamp Thing's help, Clark heals and restores his powers before flying into the sunset with a smile.

The comic allows something of an explanation about why men are four times more likely to commit suicide than women, according to the American Foundation for Suicide Prevention, and five times less likely to seek professional help when battling mental disorders such as depression, anxiety, panic attacks, and other signs of PTSD.

Clark's thoughts and actions after exposure to the deadly fungus are similar to those of male survivors who enter the Emergency Stage of the healing process for the first time. Throughout their adult life, male survivors train themselves to practice avoidance in an attempt to feel safe. However, over time, unexpected triggers remind survivors of the trauma from their past in the same way Clark becomes infected by a disease from ancient Krypton. Male survivors try to heal from the damage of childhood sexual abuse in the same way they have been socialized to handle all other problems—on their own. Male survivors believe they can identify and heal in the same way Superman investigates the alien fungus— on his own. Eventually, the facades that were developed as defense mechanisms collapse in on one another, making it impossible to control and regulate one facade from the other, just as Clark's abilities come and go without warning, merging the personalities of Clark and Superman. Although male survivors try to seclude themselves in an attempt to not hurt others, eventually they rage and self-destruct until they get the help they need to heal in the same way Swamp Thing helps to heal Superman.

Alan Moore's Superman, Clark Kent, and Swamp Thing illustrate the consequences of living a life behind a Clark Kent facade. Once triggered, the facade no longer becomes effective, and avoidance leads to rage, depression, and the possibility of self-destruction.

Without healing, the Clark Kent facade becomes unstable. Similar to Superman destroying the forest in a blind rage after crashing his car, male survivors develop self-destructive tendencies, believing they are beyond hope because they cannot heal on their own. Instead, they seclude themselves from others who care for them. They practice avoidance while also striving for human contact. Rather than seek help from others, Clark believes he is beyond healing, so he leaves to find a place to die alone. Male survivors are similar. When they avoid the trauma of sexual abuse and work through it alone, their actions only accelerate the process. This part of the book explains the origin of the Clark Kent facade, the consequences of living by the "good-guy code," and how avoidance only leads to rage and eventual self-destruction.

Chapter One: Understanding the Clark Kent Facade

"I don't want to be different. I want to be Clark Kent."

Clark Kent—*Superman: The Secret Origins of Superman* (2009)

Who is Clark Kent? Readers know and love Superman, but what about his mild-mannered alter ego? Superman is the "Man of Steel" and drawn to command attention as he streaks through the sky in the form of a red and blue comet. Clark, on the other hand, is drawn with the intention of blending into his surroundings as a pleasant but invisible "average Joe." He wears suits that are functional rather than flashy, does not raise his voice, and treats everyone (even his enemies) with respect. He never places his wants before the needs of others but remains eternally optimistic and continuously searching for ways to help and support his fellow man.

Through the eyes of many, Clark is viewed as the perfect definition of a "good guy." He is nice, respectful, but sometimes too nice for his own good. Many fans of Superman would agree that there is nothing wrong with wanting to live up to the ideals of Clark Kent. However, this portion of the book is not attempting to rid the world of this humble and likable character. Instead, it argues why you, as a male survivor, cannot perpetuate a Clark Kent facade indefinitely without eventually suffering consequences. The Clark Kent facade is unsustainable, leading to a life of loneliness and isolation.

Throughout the eighty years of the mild-mannered reporter's existence, Clark Kent has been drawn and written to be bumbling and somewhat of a pushover. Geoff Johns and Gary Frank continue this depiction in *Superman: Secret Origins* when describing Clark's arrival to Metropolis from Smallville.

Upon entering the Daily Planet building for his first day as an investigative journalist, Clark's suitcase gets jammed in the revolving door, knocking its contents (a sack lunch, a picture of his parents, papers, pens, and a picture of his dog, Krypto) to the floor. After securing each article safely in the suitcase, Clark slips on the wet, freshly mopped floor, slides through the doors of the elevator and into the pudgy chest of janitor Rudy Jones. Once inside the elevator, Rudy convinces Clark to let him have the sack lunch in the suitcase because he "forgot" his lunch at home. Later, Rudy convinces Clark to give him twenty dollars because he "forgot" his bus pass and he has no way of getting home after work.

To the reader, it is evident that the overweight janitor (soon to become the villain Parasite) is taking advantage of Clark's kindness. Unfortunately, Clark appears to be oblivious to the soon-to-be villain's true intentions. Actions and encounters similar to these between Rudy and Clark throughout *Superman* make the reporter appear to be a clumsy pushover that personifies the myth "nice guys finish last." However, Clark Kent is more than his gullibility. The true strength of Clark Kent is evident in an interaction with Lois Lane and US Army Sergeant John Corben.

Sergeant John Corben is attracted to Lois Lane and wants them to become an exclusive couple following a single failed date. While standing in a compact, messy, Daily Planet cubicle, Lois attempts to explain to Corben how she is not interested in being his friend, let alone his girlfriend. When Corben (soon to be the villain Metallo) forcefully grabs Lois by the wrist and tells her not to "dismiss" him, Clark gently places his hand on the shoulder of the decorated soldier and politely introduces himself. Rather than use force or intimidation, Clark remains true to his character and explains how he and Lois have plans for lunch. Not viewing Clark as a threat, Corben introduces himself, shakes Clark's hand, and attempts to intimidate the reporter by forcefully gripping Clark's hand to crush his knuckles. Instead, Clark's gentle smile does not waver as he tightly grips the hand of the army sergeant, crushing Corben's knuckles. He no longer presents a smug smile as he retracts his hand and immediately leaves as Clark pleasantly waves good-bye.

This interaction, and many others throughout *Superman*, is what makes Clark Kent a unique, lovable, and honorable character. Clark has the ability to remain grounded to his small-town values while remaining genuine and honest. He treats everyone as if they are someone special, in the same manner as Fred Rogers, while continuing to do what he believes is morally and ethically right rather than easy. More individuals like Clark, who attempt to accomplish what is right rather than what it easy, are needed throughout our society.

This chapter does not attempt to convince male survivors to embody the morals of Clark Kent to become "nice" men who appear weak and gullible to others. Instead, this part of the book attempts to explain why living life behind a mask of kindness denies others who care for you the opportunity to view the man behind the mask. A constant facade of pleasantries and smiles is not intimacy. It is a form of betrayal designed to keep others at an emotional distance, leading to a life of isolation and a fear of intimacy. Before understanding how to live life free from the false safety of a Clark Kent facade, it is important to know how male survivors develop the Clark Kent facade following childhood sexual abuse and how it lasts into adulthood.

Clark Kent, Smallville, and the Birth of the Facade

Clark Kent grew to become a young man while living in Smallville, Kansas. His adoptive parents, Jonathan and Martha Kent, found him in a spaceship after crash-landing to Earth from the distant, destroyed planet Krypton. Unable to have children of their own, the Kents raised Clark as their son. On the Kent's small farm in

Kansas, Jonathan and Martha instilled in Clark the small-town values of hard work and doing what was right rather than what was easy.

Throughout most of Clark's childhood, he did not have the superpowers of Superman and was ignorant of his Kryptonian heritage. Although Clark did feel as though he was different from others, rather than live a life behind the mask of three different facades, his identity remained intact. It is not until Clark's superhuman abilities began to manifest themselves throughout adolescence that the first of the three facades began to take shape, giving birth to the Clark Kent facade the night Clark came to realize he is from another planet.

Clark Kent's origin and time spent in Smallville has been told and reimagined many times over the past eighty years, but author Geoff Johns and illustrator Gary Frank do an exceptional job explaining and exploring the formation of the Clark Kent facade throughout the graphic novel *Superman: Secret Origins.* They depict the complexities involved in coming to terms with the reality of a traumatic event.

In the beginning, there is no Superman or Kal-El; there is only Clark, a boy who loves his family and playing a pickup game of football with his friends. Oblivious to the development of his super strength at the beginning of *Superman: Secret Origins*, Clark runs with a football for a touchdown. His best friend, Pete Ross, attempts to tackle Clark, but when they impact, Pete breaks his arm while Clark walks away unharmed. Ashamed and confused, Clark and Jonathan Kent drive home in relative silence, unsure of what to say, if anything. It is in this moment the Clark Kent facade begins to take shape.

The next day, while at school talking to Lana Lang (Clark's other best friend and love interest), Clark runs away in horror when he realizes he can see the fracture in Pete's arm with X-ray vision. Later, confusion and fear heighten when he starts a fire with his eyes after he and Lana kiss for the first time. When Clark returns home, feelings of shame and anxiety continue for both Clark and his father. The Clark Kent facade takes definitive shape when Jonathan and Martha reveal the truth about Clark's origins. Lifting a trapdoor in the barn, Jonathan reveals a gleaming spaceship as Martha stands beside her son. The young boy looks in awe and with a smile of amazement at the rocket that carried him to Earth. However, when he touches the cool, sleek metal, the craft opens and the holographic images of a man and woman appear. The images explain that they are Jor-El and Lara, Clark's birth parents, and that his real name is Kal-El. Clark cowers in fear as Jor-El explains why he was sent to Earth and the powers he will possess with more exposure to Earth's sun.

Finally, Jor-El tells his son, "You will be protected on this new world by the abilities its environment will provide you. And you will be free to move among the people of Earth. But never forget, although you may look like one of them, you are not one of them."

Hearing these words, Clark's eyes glow red as tears and beams of heat stream from his eyes. He punches the spaceship, telling the images to go away as he runs from the barn. Jonathan follows and holds his son when he falls. Clark cries as he asks his father, "Why did you have to show me that? Why? I don't want to be someone else. I don't want to be different. I want to be Clark Kent. I want to be your son."

Jonathan holds Clark and tells the boy, "You are my son."

In this moment the Clark Kent facade is born and the other facades of Superman and Kal-El begin to take shape. The young boy who walked into the barn no longer exists. The knowledge of the trauma of losing his planet, his birth parents, and knowing he is an alien from another planet is too much for him to handle. Rather than enter the Emergency Stage of the healing process, he copes the only way he knows how: by developing different facades of what he believes it means to be "normal." He pushes his friends Lana and

Pete away out of fear of hurting them, because he knows that, although he looks like them, he is not one of them. He does not know how to heal from this trauma or from the consequences of hiding a portion of himself from others. This results in the perfection of the facade of Clark Kent to cope and interpret what it means to be "normal" as an adult.

As a male survivor of childhood sexual abuse, it may be difficult to remember a time before the occurrence of being sexually abused. You may not remember the person you were before. In the same way, Clark finds it difficult to remember the boy he was before entering the barn to see the spaceship that carried him to Earth and before knowing he was different. You may believe there was never a time before the occurrence of the sexual abuse, and, like Clark, you believe you are damaged and different from other men because of a belief that men and boys cannot be sexually abused when, in fact, one in six men will be sexually abused in their lifetime, and 16 percent of boys are sexually assaulted before the age of eighteen, according to the Center for Disease Control. You may believe there was never a time when you felt safe and secure with who you were, rather than being alone and afraid of the person you had become. Similar to Clark, you, as a male survivor, may view yourself as a "freak" and push those closest to you away out of fear of hurting them because you believe deep down you are bad, evil, and flawed. Clark does this in *Superman: Secret Origin* when he pushes away his best friends Lana Lang and Pete Ross after discovering the origin of his superpowers.

In *Superman: Secret Origin*, Clark stops playing football out of fear that he will hurt others in the same way he hurt Pete. Rather than agree to play after school, Clark makes excuses. He tells his friends he has bad allergies, a stomachache, a dentist appointment, or that he does not want to get wet in the rain, yet it's a clear day without a cloud in the sky. Pete offers the quarterback position to Clark to ensure limited contact with others, but still Clark says no. Saddened, Clark watches as his former friends walk toward the football field while making fun of his glasses. None of the boys (including Pete) know Clark has super abilities. He lies in an attempt to do what he believes will keep them safe.

While Clark pushes Pete away, he also pushes away Lana Lang for similar yet different reasons. Throughout *Superman: Secret Origin*, Lana makes it apparent that she has a crush on him. It is also evident that Clark feels the same way when he enters a tornado to save Lana's life as she is lifted from the ground. With the tornado debris for cover, Clark flies for the first time and the two crash-land in a nearby stream. Afterward the two kiss, and Clark's eyes glow red from the excitement.

Later, when Clark tells Lana that Pete is no longer asking him to play football, he questions any friendship he may have if he can't tell the truth about who he is and what he can do. These thoughts and feelings not only apply to Pete, but Lana as well, because he tells Lana half-truths about who he truly is and where he came from. While Lana knows Clark has special abilities, Clark will not tell her the source of his powers is from the sun and that he is an alien from a different planet. Clark will not tell her the truth out of fear of how she may view him afterward. He is afraid of being labeled a "freak" by the friend he cares for. He is also afraid of hurting her with his abilities. It is for all of these reasons that when Lana leans in to kiss Clark on the cheek and his eyes began to glow red, Clark pushes the young girl away, telling her, "I'm not looking for anything more than a friend." Angry and hurt, Lana walks away, and Clark is left standing alone, listening to the distant whispers of kids he used to call his friends.

Similar to Clark, you, as a male survivor, may be afraid of the impact your childhood sexual abuse will have on your current relationships if the sexual abuse is ever discovered. You may believe that the anger, anxiety, confusion, and fear you feel and your attempt to keep this pushed down will somehow become unleashed like Clark's heat vision, hurting others in the same way you were hurt. Similar to Clark, the childhood sexual abuse may also make you feel like a "freak" from a different planet. In the same way Clark feels alone because he is the only Kryptonian on the planet (he knows about), you may feel just as isolated from others because of the perpetuated belief that men and boys cannot be sexually abused. So, similar to Clark, you push away those closest to you and those you care for the most. You tell lies and half-truths to keep others at a distance, perfecting the Clark Kent facade and never truly showing intimacy. Over time, with enough practice, the facade no longer becomes a mask. The lies become truth. Similar to the way Pete no longer asked Clark to play football, you and others will forget the person you were prior to the trauma of being sexually abused.

There are a number of reasons why survivors feel they must perpetuate the Clark Kent facade in order to feel safe. Arielle Schwartz, PhD, explains that the core problem with survivors of complex PTSD such as childhood sexual abuse and assault is that while survivors long for connection and intimate relationships in the same way Clark Kent wanted to be friends with Pete Ross and Lana Lang, these feelings conflict with beliefs and memories that relationships aren't safe. Clark's feelings of confusion and loss can be seen in his fear of being truly intimate with those closest to him. Over time, male survivors develop a Clark Kent facade to minimize feelings of loneliness, isolation, and the possibility of threat.

Like Clark, male survivors attempt to hide in plain sight. In *Superman: Secret Origin*, Clark wore glasses and stopped playing football. He remained silent, afraid of being the villain he believed he had the possibility of becoming if he revealed his abilities and expressed his feelings of anger over being different. Many male survivors also attempt to hide their feelings of fear and pain by remaining silent and keeping others at a distance. Male survivors learn it is the only way to ensure their safety. Unfortunately, as an adult survivor, the Clark Kent facade ensures limited intimacy by distancing others and by people pleasing. This pushes others away and creates a hollow shell of a complete individual.

Clark Kent, Metropolis, and Perpetuating the Clark Kent Facade

Male survivors who mature into adulthood and continue to hide behind a Clark Kent facade often sacrifice happiness in exchange for safety. This is demonstrated in *Superman: Earth One*, when Clark visits the grave of his father, Jonathan Kent. His words provide a good understanding of why many male survivors feel the need to sacrifice happiness to feel safe. With tears in his eyes, Clark tells his father:

I can get a good job. A creative job that'll pay me more money than I can spend in a lifetime. Enough money to let me honor the promise I made while you were dying in my arms, to always look after Mom. And I can be happy. All my life, I've been alone. I was alone as a kid because I didn't know how to pretend to fit in. No matter what I did they could sense I was different. I didn't have a choice. But now I do have a choice. Now I know how to fit in. How to pretend to be just one of the guys and I want that. I want that bad. If I expose myself to the world, if I show them what I can do, I'll always be on the run. I'll never fit in. I'll always be on the outside looking in. I'll be alone. Worse still, I'll have made the choice to be alone. I couldn't make that choice before, but I can now. And I choose to be happy. To have a life. And isn't that what you said you wanted most? For me to be happy?

Here, Clark explains how being different means not being happy. He explains while hovering over the grave of his father that being unique and being Superman would mean he would forever be alone without a life or friends of his own. Clark believes that in order to be happy and to have a life he must hide part of himself from others.

Unfortunately, Clark is not alone in his beliefs. Many male survivors of sexual abuse share similar beliefs about themselves and their happiness. They shield themselves behind a Clark Kent facade and believe that if they are ever going to be truly happy, they must fit in and hide a part of themselves to please others. For male survivors, this means denying they were sexually abused as a child and becoming what society expects boys and men to become.

However, what Clark Kent and many male survivors do not know is that living life behind a Clark Kent facade can be lonelier than a life behind a Superman facade. This is because both the Superman and the Clark Kent facades perpetuate a lie from childhood into adulthood that makes survivors feel alone no matter if they are surrounded by friends, family, and loved ones.

Living a life behind the facade of Clark Kent also means never truly becoming intimate. Lacking intimacy as a survivor means no one meets the man behind the mask and never being present when others need you the most. Clark demonstrates this lack of intimacy when he leaves Smallville and begins his career as a journalist in Metropolis.

In Metropolis, Clark no longer has his friends Lana Lang and Pete Ross. Instead, he has his colleagues Lois Lane, Jimmy Olson, and Perry White. As a boy, Clark found it difficult to maintain a facade to keep others at a distance and ignorant of the person hiding behind the glasses. However, as an adult, Clark has perfected his facade—he falls, slips, is nice, straightlaced, and somewhat gullible. Although Clark is in contact with fellow reporter (and eventual wife) Lois Lane, photographer (and coffee boy) Jimmy Olsen, and Perry White (editor of the *Daily Planet*) every day of his adult life, none of them suspect Clark Kent is also Superman. This is not because of Clark's glasses and cheap suit, but because as an adult Clark's facade is no longer a facade. Instead, he is a complete individual separate from Superman with his own needs, wants, beliefs, and thoughts regardless of how similar their appearance. The actuality of Clark Kent's facade is seen in episode two of Grant Morrison's *All-Star Superman*, "Superman's Forbidden Room."

In the graphic novel, Superman is dying from the supersaturation of his cells with yellow sunlight. The Man of Steel knows he does not have much time left to live, so Clark decides to reveal to Lois Lane that he is Superman. Before Lois's eyes, he rips apart the buttons of his shirt to reveal the iconic red and yellow "S," removes his glasses, and flies Lois (while sitting in her car) to the doors of the Fortress of Solitude in the North Pole. Although all of this should prove, beyond the shadow of a doubt, that Clark Kent is Superman, Lois refuses to believe they are the same person.

While sitting down to dinner in the Fortress of Solitude, Lois goes through each scenario in which Clark was seen in the same room as Superman. For each moment, whether it be a robot double or Batman standing in, Superman has an explanation, and still she refuses to believe the truth. She cannot and will not accept that Clark and Superman are one and the same when she says, "What if there really was some part of him that was bumbling, oafish Clark Kent? I just don't know if I could live with that."

Clark has lied to Lois for years. She has questioned numerous times whether Clark and Superman were one and the same. Finally, when confronted with the truth, Lois cannot believe her own eyes. It is too far-fetched for Lois to believe that Clark does not exist, and this is the tragedy of the Clark Kent facade. If you, as a survivor, hide who you are long enough, the false identity eventually becomes a reality that is difficult to erase. The mask of the facade no longer becomes fake, it becomes the truth after years of learning to exist and hide in plain sight. The next chapter further explains the consequences of maintaining the Clark Kent facade as an adult.

Chapter Two: Consequences of the Clark Kent Facade

"I must tell her my secret identity–then give up my Superman career and remain only in my Clark Kent identity!"

Clark Kent—*Superman #129* (1959), "The Girl in Superman's Past"

In *All-Star Superman* (2011), "Episode 5: The Gospel According to Lex Luthor," Lex Luthor has been sentenced to death by electric chair for his continuous schemes and plots to kill Superman. Clark Kent visits Lex in prison to write and publish the villain's final testimony for the *Daily Planet*. While in prison, Lex is allowed to continue experimenting, exercising, and moving about the common area as he wishes, but with continuous armed escort.

Upon entering Lex's workshop, the villain tells Clark, "Yes, I'm aware of your lumbering presence, Kent," as the disguised superhero trips over Lex's tool, saving the evil scientist from electrocution and maintaining the facade of a bumbling fool. As Clark fixes his glasses and spills paper across the floor, Lex says, "Look at you! You write like a poet, but you move like a landslide."

Clark does not become angry at the insult and Lex never says thank you to Clark for saving his life as the two enter the gym. Here the weak and complacent facade of Clark Kent is juxtaposed beside the arrogant and domineering personality of Lex Luthor. Lex runs with weights as Clark writes. From the treadmill, Lex goes to dead lifts. All the while, Lex criticizes Clark's use of shorthand rather than using a tape recorder, telling the reporter that without Superman, Clark may have had a chance with Lois Lane. He tells Clark:

Imagine life on this world if some opportunistic alien vermin hadn't decided to dump its trash here, Kent. That's all I've ever asked anyone to do. Imagine how it was meant to be. Think about it, without Superman to distract her, you just never know. Perhaps cool, cruel Lois Lane might actually have noticed good old Clark, sighing faithfully there in the corner. I'm just saying a tall, strapping midwestern farmer's boy with brains, integrity, and no style of his own? That's a prize catch for any cynical city gal. Throw in some weight training and that flabby physique of yours could even come to rival Superman's build. But next to him she sees an oak, a dullard, a cripple! Next to "All-Powerful Superman," Lex Luthor is an idiot. And you know what, Kent? She'll never see past him to you!

Lex finishes the monologue by throwing his weights at Clark, telling the reporter to feel his muscles. Here, Lex insults both Clark and his alter ego, Superman. He acknowledges Clark's invisibility, loneliness, and feelings of isolation he has felt throughout his entire life. However, Clark's facade remains intact. Clark does not become angry or depressed. Instead, he continues to keep his head down while writing, accomplishing his job with the knowledge that this is the way the world works and the belief that the code he has lived his life by remains intact, allowing the feeling of safety and assurance that everything will turn out all right in the end.

Afterward, Clark and Lex enter the common yard where the villain Parasite is being returned to his cell. Unfortunately, because Clark Kent is secretly Superman, Parasite grows stronger, breaks free, and causes a riot throughout the prison. To maintain the facade of mild-mannered and invisible Clark Kent, the reporter feigns cowardice as Lex remains calm, confident, and ignorant in his ability to remain unharmed. The facade of Clark has become so perfected, he is able to enter the tear gas spread by the officers, stumble into an inmate who holds a gun to the back of Lex's head, remove all the officers from the prison, use his heat vision to activate the sprinklers, freeze the rioting prisoners with his ice breath, and make Lex believe he led them to safety without a single mishap.

It is not until Lex and Clark return to Lex Luthor's cell that Clark loses his grip on the facade. Inside the cell, Lex reveals to Clark how he has built a secret tunnel leading out of the prison using one of his inventions. Silently descending the steps, Clark cleans his glasses before questioning Lex about why he is still in prison if he could have escaped at any time. The villain tells Clark, "I am going to the chair fulfilled." He knows Superman will die, and that is all he cares about.

Clark speaks calmly before screaming in rage, "I can't believe you're getting ready to die like this. You and Superman could have been friends! You'll die like a mad dog in the yard! Think straight, Lex!"

Clark's words have no effect on the villain. Luthor hates Superman and is pleased that the hero will die. Ashamed at his outburst and lost as to what to do next, Clark places the glasses back on his face and looks back on Lex with remorse as he is taken to safety.

Clark's actions in *All-Star Superman* are an excellent example of the cycle of avoidance, becoming triggered, and the resulting feelings of depression and low self-worth many male survivors experience when attempting to live a life behind a Clark Kent facade. This chapter attempts to explain the consequences which can lead to attempting to live a life by the rules of the good-guy code.

The Good-Guy Code, Avoidance, Anger, and Depression

Male survivors develop the Clark Kent facade as a result of being unable to assert appropriate boundaries for their feelings and expectations. These survivors lack interpersonal effectiveness. They lack an ability to build positive self-respect for themselves and lack a sense of self-worth. Arielle Schwartz, PhD, explains how this means having an unbounded boundary style in *The Complex PTSD Workbook*.

In the workbook, Schwartz explains how survivors who have an unbounded boundary style tend to merge their thoughts, feelings, and beliefs with others around them, losing a sense of themselves for the sake of building relationships. Their inability to identify and be honest about their limits have the possibility of leading to resentment and anger for feeling as though they must take care of others rather than care for themselves.

If viewed through the lens of **Internal Family System (IFS) Therapy**, as discussed in the introduction, the Clark Kent facade represents the *exile*, a portion of a survivor's identity that is attempting to reintegrate with the self. Similar to Clark carrying the burden of being the only Kryptonian on Earth, male survivors carry the burden of believing they are the only (or one of the few) boys or men who have ever been sexually abused, assaulted, or raped. These boys and men feel isolated and alone when, like Clark, they just want to fit in. Many male survivors mask these feelings and beliefs behind a Clark Kent facade. They feel this way because of a society that perpetuates a belief that men and boys cannot be sexually abused, assaulted, or raped. The *exile* portion of the self feels isolated and filled with shame, attempts to be happy to please others, and believes this will make them happy as well.

Exiles hate themselves for being different, and so hate their inner child. They blame their inner child for being different. This is seen in the boy Clark was upon entering the barn with his parents, and the boy he became after exiting and viewing the rocket which carried him to Earth from Krypton.

When Clark Kent entered the barn with Jonathan and Marth Kent after the manifestation of his super abilities, he had no reason to hate his inner child. He believed himself to be a normal Midwestern boy with two loving parents. After leaving the barn and viewing the rocket, everything changed. In those few moments, he realized he was the last of a dead race who had been raised by two people he loved but who were not his biological parents. After exiting the barn, he developed the exile portion of his identity, which hated being different, and himself for a traumatic event he had no ability to control. Similar to Clark, before being sexually abused, male survivors are complete with an intact inner child. Afterward, they develop the exile portion of the self who hates themselves for being different, weak, and not strong enough to stop the trauma they had no control in preventing.

Survivors with an inability to create limits and boundaries create the Clark Kent facade as a defense mechanism when childhood trauma and abuse is inescapable. Rather than *fight-or-flight*, these survivors *freeze-and-collapse*. Bessel van Der Kolk explains in *The Body Keeps the Score* how this may develop when the perpetrator of the sexual abuse is a close relative, friend, or partner. The proximity to the survivor's day-to-day interactions with their abusers make escape an impossibility. It is for this reason, when survivors no longer have the ability to *fight-or-flight*, that they attempt to minimize the impact of their abuse by attempting to appease and read the mind of their abuser. These survivors become hyperaroused in the same way Clark begins to develop the ability to almost read the thoughts of others with his super hearing. *Freeze-and-collapse* forces a survivor to read the minds of their abuser, ignoring their own needs and limits, in an attempt to become as safe as possible in a hostile environment. Judith Herman goes on to explain the need of a survivor to *freeze-and-collapse* in her book *Trauma and Recovery* when she writes:

Adaptation to this climate of constant danger requires a state of constant alertness. Children in an abusive environment develop extraordinary abilities to scan for warning signs of attack. They become minutely attuned to their abusers' inner states. They learn to recognize subtle changes in facial expression, voice, and body language as signals of anger, sexual arousal, intoxication, or dissociation. This nonverbal

35

communication becomes highly automatic and occurs for the most part outside of conscious awareness.

As a child, this ability to put their own needs and wants aside ensures their survival. However, as an adult, when a safe environment has been achieved, the Clark Kent facade results in an inability to set boundaries for themselves. These individuals become labeled as "people pleasers," morphing their emotions to match those of others they are in a relationship with. Others are placed first, creating a male survivor who follows the good-guy code.

Male survivors who mask themselves behind a Clark Kent facade fear they may become the abuser of someone else in the same manner they were sexually abused, so they practice avoidance, doing all they can with a smile and a laugh to avoid feelings of isolation, anxiety, and shame. Unfortunately, when triggered and unable to manage their emotions, rage and fear become inescapable, creating a grip of panic and fear. Afterward, when unable to live up to the good-guy code they create for themselves, male survivors become depressed, feeling powerless, as if they have become the monster they feared they would become. These feelings can lead to thoughts of self-harm and possible attempts of suicide.

Clark's actions in *All-Star Superman* are an excellent example demonstrating the cycle of emotions outlined in **Dialectical Behavior Therapy (DBT)**. Male survivors who identify with the Clark Kent facade lack *interpersonal effectiveness*. This means that male survivors practice avoidance to control their emotions. Male survivors may suppress their feelings of anger, sadness, and anxiety in the same manner as Clark Kent did toward Lex Luthor while in prison. Rather than discuss his thoughts, beliefs, and disapproval of Lex's actions and thoughts throughout "The Gospel According to Lex Luthor," Clark let his thoughts and emotions build until his feelings exploded in rage. Many male survivors who live by the good-guy code live by similar rules of keeping their thoughts and emotions bottled until, similar to a shaken bottle of soda, they have no choice but to explode from the pressure. When this occurs, male survivors believe they have violated their own unwritten laws to always remain calm and, as a result, become depressed. Clark demonstrates his rapid progression from rage to remorse as he cowardly gets into the boat and drifts away to safety. In the moment Clark lost his temper, he believed himself, not Lex, to be the villain, hating himself for not having the ability to control his emotions.

This is the consequence of living behind the mask of the Clark Kent facade. Male survivors believe themselves to be the villain and view themselves as a perpetrator of abuse and assault when triggered and unable to suppress their emotions any longer. When avoidance is no longer effective, they become withdrawn and depressed, hating themselves and seeking safety in the same manner as Mister Mxyzptlk in the DC comic event, *Superman Rebirth*.

Mister Mxyzptlk and Establishing Safety

The Clark Kent facade is not worn only by Clark Kent, it is also the mask assumed by the short, bald, top-hatted, fifth-dimensional magical trickster Mister Mxyzptlk following his escape from a mysterious green-hooded being wielding a double-bladed scythe in *Superman: Rebirth*. After being imprisoned in a cell between dimensions, Mxyzptlk did not attempt to escape his captor when first imprisoned. Instead, he decided to wait. He was certain "his pal, Superman" would soon arrive to save the day. Mxyzptlk assumed that because Superman was the greatest hero of all time and had saved other villains worse than himself from far worse circumstances, all he needed to do was bide his time and the Big Blue Boy Scout would arrive to save the day. Unfortunately, he was wrong. Superman did not know Mxyzptlk was captured and so did not know the trickster needed to be saved. Realizing he is alone without the possibility of rescue, he feels powerless for the first time in his existence and experiences true fear. The overwhelming fear and isolation drives the trickster mad.

Eventually, Mxyzptlk is able to escape using the magic created from saying his own name backward multiple times. Once free, the only way he knows to hide is by transforming (mind, body, and spirit) into someone else. The person he chooses to embody is Clark Kent. To fully assume the role of the *Daily Planet* reporter, the trickster erases his own memory and replaces it with what he knows of Clark. When this occurs, Mxyzptlk believes he *is* Clark Kent, a reporter for the *Daily Planet* who was born and raised on a small farm in Smallville, Kansas, while the real Clark Kent still exists in reality. Unlike the real Clark Kent, Mxyzptlk did not incorporate the memories of Krypton and of arriving to Earth in a spaceship. He was *only* Clark Kent, embodying the Clark Kent facade to create a sense of safety that was stripped away when he was imprisoned between dimensions.

Throughout the comic, Mxyzptlk behaves as he believes Clark would behave, but with more childish tendencies. He bumbles his way through life, ruining stories and stakeouts, eating nothing but junk food, and claiming to live in Clark's old apartment at 344 Clinton Ave. The fifth-dimensional being even confesses his love for Lois Lane (who is already married to the real Clark) and asks her to marry him after their first date because he believes that is what he is *supposed* to do to perpetuate the facade and continue feeling safe. After Lois rejects his offer of marriage, Mxyzptlk sees Lois with the real Clark and their son, Jonathan, causing all the memories of his past imprisonment to return with the truth of his identity. In a wave of anxiety, fear, and shock, Clark's doppelganger stands outside the window of the Kent farm, watching the family enjoy their dinner, and says to himself, "It's . . . it's all coming back to me. I remember. I remember all of it. You've ruined my life. Ruined everything!"

As Clark Kent, Mister Mxyzptlk embodied the Clark Kent facade in an attempt to avoid the fear he felt while imprisoned and feeling powerless for the first time in his existence. Rather than confront the past to heal, Mister Mxyzptlk attempts to regain a sense of safety by assuming the Clark Kent facade. Unfortunately, when avoidance is no longer an option, Mxyzptlk becomes triggered when the reality of his past returns, making him no longer feel safe and in control of his life. Once triggered and no longer able to hide behind the facade of Clark Kent, Mxyzptlk becomes angry, projecting his hatred and rage on individuals he once loved and who he feels are responsible for bringing an end to his perfect reality: the Kent family. Seeking revenge, Mister Mxyzptlk (in the form of Clark Kent) attempts to bring an end to Clark's happiness. While celebrating Jonathan's birthday, Mister Mxyzptlk erases Clark's past in a torrent of white flames that eventually erase the memory of Jonathan from existence.

As a male survivor of childhood sexual abuse, the consequence of attempting to maintain a false facade of Clark Kent means that, eventually, the facade will take on a life of its own in the same way Superman's alter ego appears to come to life to Clark and Lois. If left to exist long enough, the facade will fight for its existence as any other living creature would fight to live. The only difference between Mxyzptlk, Clark Kent, and yourself is that this battle of the facade will occur internally. If you, as a male survivor, choose to maintain your Clark Kent facade into adulthood, the life you have built, meant to be perfect, predictable, and dependable, will eventually crumble and slip through your fingers. Sooner or later you will become triggered. Avoidance will no longer be an option. Feelings of shame, fear, sadness, powerlessness, and anxiety will come rushing back as you enter the Emergency Stage. To cope with these emotions, you will become angry, anxious, and hypervigilant, lashing out at those you love, tearing down the dependable reality you built to feel safe, in the same manner as Mister Mxyzptlk attacking the real Clark Kent. If left unchecked, these feelings will lead to a belief that you have broken the good-guy code, causing feelings of depression, further avoidance, and a continuation of the cycle that will strengthen the need for the Clark Kent facade. Conquering the Clark Kent facade means acquiring the tools needed to establish a true sense of safety that is effective in navigating the flood of emotions associated with entering the Emergency Stage of the healing process. Without establishing a sense of safety, you will always believe there is a need for the Clark Kent facade, no matter how strong or good you may believe yourself to be. This is the only way to conquer the need for a Clark Kent facade.

Chapter Three: Conquering the Clark Kent Facade

"You aren't Superman, but you're not even Clark Kent anymore. You gotta stop waiting for something to happen and start living in the RIGHT NOW, 'cause every second that you don't you're letting us all down!"

Pete Ross—*Superman: American Alien (2017)*

The smile dissolves from the happy-go-lucky, clean-shaven face of the Kansas farmer and is replaced with the hard-set eyes, clenched jaw, and steel-like focus of a distant call for help. In an instant, the mild-mannered reporter snatches the wire-rimmed glasses from his face as a small lock of hair falls, curls, and rests in the center of his forehead in the form of a miniaturized "S." In one fluid motion and with blinding speed, the buttoned shirt separates to reveal the Kryptonian symbol for hope on a background of gold. As the Man of Steel takes to the sky with ease, he announces as if preparing himself for danger or to warn evildoers of his approaching arrival, "This looks like a job for Superman!"

These are the words lovers of *Superman* yearn to read. In this moment, readers know good is rising to conquer evil. They know Superman will arrive, outwit the villain with his strength or speed, and all will be right with the world. In this moment, readers encounter Superman and forget the Big Blue Boy Scout ever had a mild-mannered alter ego. They know when there is a job for Superman, but what about Clark Kent? When (if ever) is there a job for Clark Kent? Why or when is Smallville needed to rise to the occasion? More often than readers may realize.

While Superman is known to swoop in, save the day, and disappear without a trace, Clark Kent provides readers and his friends with a sense of security and dependability that is more constant than the Man of Steel. Although Lois Lane, Jimmy Olson, and Perry White may not know where Clark vanishes when danger arises, they know he will be there when the smoke clears to help put the pieces of the city (and their lives) back together. Knowing this makes Clark Kent's character safe and dependable. Others lean on him for support, knowing he is a character they can trust just as much (if not more) than Superman. It is for this reason some male survivors attempt to hide who they are behind a Clark Kent facade rather than the facade of Kal-El or Superman.

Following sexual assault as children, male survivors live in a constant state of fear and unpredictability. Most male survivors find it difficult to trust others out of fear of being hurt in the same manner they were hurt by their abuser. Male survivors do not trust their thoughts due to the shame perpetuated by society that because they are boys and men they cannot be sexually abused, assaulted, or raped. Their mistrust is compounded by their belief that they were betrayed by their body when they reacted to physical stimuli, which may have resulted in an erection or ejaculation. Male survivors live in a constant state of fear in and around their body. To establish a sense of safety, some male survivors develop the Clark Kent facade to provide order to a chaotic world by living by the rules of their own good-guy code. They also develop the Clark Kent facade and live by their good-guy code in the hopes that they will not become the villain they believe themselves to be due to the shame associated with being a male survivor. These rules create boxes and categorizations that provide a black-and-white view of the world (similar to a comic), making it easy to simplify the identification of heroes, villains, success, and failure. When an anomaly occurs in the logic of their good-guy code, male survivors of the Clark Kent facade practice avoidance, bottling their emotions until triggered. Once triggered, male survivors no longer feel safe because the world no longer abides by the good-guy code of their creation. To cope they become angry and frustrated. Unfortunately, their expression of rage makes them believe they have become the villain they feared they would become. Afterward, feelings of depression, anxiety, and fear dominate, making the male survivor believe they have violated the rules of the good-guy code. The only way to conquer the need for the Superman facade is to establish a sense of safety that was never established in childhood.

Physical, Mental, and Emotional Safety

Safety is the most important factor when choosing to heal from the trauma of childhood sexual abuse. Without a sense of safety and security, the work of creating a survivor's narrative to understand the nature of childhood sexual abuse is not sustainable. In fact, if a survivor does not feel safe when attempting to practice mindfulness or meditation, it can cause more harm than good.

What is safety? What does it mean to be safe? There are three different ways a survivor can find a sense of safety: *physical*, *mental*, and *emotional*.

Physical safety is when the body is no longer in danger. If physical danger is present, a survivor who is physically safe can either protect or remove themselves from the situation. Survivors of homes where domestic violence was (or is) a consistent threat may find it difficult to heal in a place that does not put them at ease. There is the persistent threat of fight-or-flight or freeze-and-collapse. *Mental safety* means having the ability to remain grounded, centered, and focused on their own thoughts and feelings without dissociating from reality. *Emotional safety* means having the ability to control and regulate feelings without consistently experiencing hyperarousal and being plunged into panic attacks.

All three of these forms of safety interact with one another, oftentimes making it difficult (or even impossible) for a survivor to differentiate between their body, mind, and emotions. Fulfilling each measure of safety requires acquiring and utilizing a different set of tools. Male survivors of childhood sexual abuse who have developed a Clark Kent facade often find it difficult to identify when and if they are safe (let alone which form of safety) because they live in an inescapable environment of fear.

When identifying your own level of safety as a male survivor of childhood sexual abuse, authors Williams and Poijula explain in *The PTSD Handbook* how it is important to ask yourself eleven simple questions when attempting to gauge a sense of safety. It would be helpful to keep a journal of your responses to return to and track how your responses either change over time or remain the same. If at any time you feel triggered or overwhelmed when answering the questions, put this guide down and return when you are comfortable. Remember, healing is not a race but a journey. Give yourself time.

Safety Questions

1. How safe is your environment? Is your home safe? Why/why not?

2. What makes you feel physically safe when you are alone? With others? In different situations?

3. Are those with whom you live or interact safe? If they are, what makes the setting and those people safe? If they are not, what makes them unsafe?

4. If you are not safe at home, is there anything you can do to increase your sense of safety?

5. If you are not safe with or around those closest to you, what will make your situation safer?

6. How can you (and how do you) protect yourself?

7. How successful are you at physically protecting yourself?

8. When are you physically the safest?

9. When do you mentally and emotionally feel the safest?

10. How can you protect yourself when you are with people you do not know?

11. What do your answers to these questions tell you about you and your sense of safety?

Subjective Units of Distress Scale (SUDS)

Another manner to assess your level of safety is with the **subjective units of distress scale (SUDS),** developed by Dr. Larry Smyth in 1997. The scale has eleven points and is a simple way to communicate your level of distress, safety, and anxiety to yourself or when speaking with a therapist, counselor, or psychiatrist. The scale was later modified for survivors of complex PTSD to lead them from feelings of numbness or extreme rage to a safe regulation of emotions. The second scale will be further discussed in part three, "The Kal-El Facade." The SUDS scale below has been modified to associate the levels of discomfort to Clark Kent and his possible levels of distress.

Numeric Rating	Description
Zero	You feel like Clark Kent living in Smallville before acquiring his super abilities to hear the conversations of everyone on the planet. Like Clark, you are at peace. You feel completely relaxed. Almost as if you are in a deep sleep. You have no distress, anxiety, or discomfort at all.
One	You feel like Clark Kent while living in either Smallville or Metropolis on a good night, when the world, the people, and its problems seem at ease. You are awake, but you feel very relaxed. Your mind wanders and drifts, similar to what you might feel just prior to falling asleep.
Two	You feel like Clark Kent alone in his apartment, no longer feeling the weight of pretending to be mild-mannered or super. The facade has dropped. You are

	relaxed, comfortable, and in a safe place physically, mentally, and emotionally. You may feel this way when at home watching television, reading a comic book, or relaxing on a calm afternoon.
Three	You feel like Clark Kent walking along the sidewalk of Metropolis without Lois Lane or Jimmy Olson at your side. There are other people present on the sidewalk, but they are strangers. There is no need to maintain a facade because there is no one present who knows who you are beneath your facade. However, the facade is still present, and, like Clark, there is still the slight discomfort of your costume brushing against your earth-toned suit, reminding you of the ever-present possibility of danger. You feel tension, but only enough to keep your attention. There is no severe discomfort, but it is also not pleasant.
Four	You feel like Clark Kent sitting at his desk at the *Daily Planet* working on a story. There is very little effort needed to maintain the facade, but the presence and movement of so many people make the possibility of thinking straight and with ease an impossibility out of fear that someone will discover your secret. You feel a mild sense of tension and discomfort that is not pleasant but is manageable.
Five	You feel like Clark Kent walking through the bustling office of the *Daily Planet*. The pressure of maintaining the facade of a bumbling reporter raised on a farm is felt, but not too intense. The added pressure of maintaining hyperarousal as Superman and the fear that others will discover your secret make it hard to stay focused and grounded on the present. Like Clark, you feel a mild sense of distress. You are uncomfortable, possibly causing some amount of dissociation, but the distress is still able to be managed.

Six	You feel like Clark Kent being confronted by Lois Lane saying that she knows you are Superman. She has not seen who you are behind your facade, and you know how to convince others that the facade is real, but the stress of putting the plan into motion and making the lie believable makes it difficult to focus. Like Clark, you have very unpleasant feelings of anxiety, anger, worry, and apprehension, but you are still able to think clearly.
Seven	You feel like Superman during an intense fight with a strong metahuman like Parasite. The punches hurt and knock you off balance, but you are still able to stand and keep fighting for the most part. Like Clark, you have a somewhat high level of distress that makes it difficult to concentrate and perform normally.
Eight	You feel like Superman being bombarded with magic. It is not as painful as kryptonite, but, like Clark, you have high levels of distress, fear, anxiety, worry, apprehension, and/or bodily tension. Thinking and problem-solving are extremely difficult. Your bodily distress is substantial. Your ability to do everyday functions is difficult and seemingly impossible.
Nine	You feel like Superman exposed to a small portion of kryptonite. The high levels of extreme distress make it nearly impossible to think clearly. Like Superman, you may even be bombarded with possible thoughts of death or your mortality as the pain seems to never stop.
Ten	You feel like Superman being bombarded with high levels of concentrated kryptonite. Like Superman, you are under extreme distress. The feelings of anxiety, fear, apprehension, and shame are the most intense you can imagine. The pain makes it impossible to stand, move, or think clearly.

Grounding

When attempting to establish a sense of safety, a beneficial tool is learning to ground yourself. Similar to the way a tree's roots keep it connected to the earth in the midst of a raging storm, grounding helps you focus your attention on the present when beginning to dissociate from reality. It is as simple as focusing on your breathing or the feeling of material against your skin to allow the mind to return to the present. There are many different forms of grounding as means of practicing mindfulness, but one that is simple and effective when beginning to dissociate is to focus in on and identify:

- Five things you see
- Four things you feel
- Three things you hear
- Two things you smell
- One thing you taste

This activity will help remind you as a male survivor that you are safe and present within your body.

Creating a Safe Place

When beginning the work to heal and conquer a Clark Kent facade, it is important to create a place where you feel you are allowed to think, behave, and feel comfortable without the pressure of judgment—a Fortress of Solitude to escape the harsh realities of the world. When creating my safe place, this is what my therapist, Susan Todd LCSW-C, told me:

> When we were young, we had our places we went to get away from what was bothering us, somewhere we could sit in peace without siblings or adults having access to us. When we sat down in this safe place, we always felt good. It's in this place we were able to play with the objects of childhood. There we could think our thoughts and say our words out loud, without anyone telling us, judging us, or pushing us. That was the wisdom of childhood.

Now you can call on that same wisdom. Find or create a safe place for yourself now. A place just for you, not for sharing with anyone else. Your paradise. Spend scheduled time there at first. In the future, you will be drawn to your safe space naturally. There you can rest, heal, hide, think, play, and get yourself ready to go back out and be your best.

Creating a safe place is vital to your recovery. It is in this place that you will meditate, reflect, and center yourself. Without this safe place, there can be no true growth and no inner peace.

Mindfulness and Meditation

Feeling safe mentally can sometimes be the most important form of safety that affects the other forms of safety, making mindfulness and meditation so important. Practicing these strategies centers and calms the mind, allowing the survivor to acquire the tools needed to feel safe in their body when physical safety may not be an option.

A strategy that is helpful throughout all stages of the healing process is learning to meditate, which allows time for thoughts to mature, the mind to rest, and the body to relax. To many, beginning to meditate seems impossible, but like all other activities it takes practice to master. To understand different meditation techniques, you may want to seek out classes, research, and watch videos on the Internet to master this developing skill. As you begin this process, note that there is no goal to be reached. Instead, meditation requires a calm mind. Below are three different meditation strategies you can use.

Stairs:

Create a safe place.

While in your safe place, sit comfortably for fifteen minutes. If you feel comfortable doing so, play relaxing sounds for meditation. For example, nature sounds of crashing waves or falling rain.

Close your eyes and breathe slowly. Take deep breaths in through your nose and out through your mouth.

Picture ten steps in your mind. These steps can be of any style and you feel comfortable imagining them.

Imagine numbers on each step descending from ten at the top to one at the bottom. The color of the paint and steps is your choice.

See yourself carefully walking backward down each step one at a time.

As you descend, continue to breathe deeply in through your nose and out through your mouth. With each step, you should feel yourself becoming more at rest and your mind at ease.

When you reach the bottom of the steps, continue to breathe while allowing your mind to wander and unwind on its own for the remainder of the fifteen minutes.

At the end of the fifteen minutes, slowly ascend the steps until you return to your body.

Progressive Relaxation:

Create a safe place.

While in your safe place, sit comfortably for fifteen minutes. If you feel comfortable doing so, play relaxing sounds for meditation. For example, nature sounds of crashing waves or falling rain.

Close your eyes and breathe slowly. Take deep breaths in through your nose and out through your mouth.

Very slowly, beginning at your toes, tense your muscles. Do this very slowly, all the way to the top of your head. Slowly relax your muscles, starting at your head all the way down to your toes.

Repeat tensing and relaxing your muscles for the remainder of the fifteen minutes (at least three to five times).

Neon Light:

Create a safe place. While in your safe place, sit comfortably for fifteen minutes. If you feel comfortable doing so, play relaxing sounds for meditation. For example, nature sounds of crashing waves or falling rain.

Close your eyes and breathe slowly. Take deep breaths in through your nose and out through your mouth.

Imagine a neon ring. The color of the ring is your choice.

Imagine the neon ring loosely encircling your ankles. The ring does not hurt but has a sense of healing radiating outward and into your skin.

Slowly imagine the neon ring extending up your body, expanding and retracting to match the shape and form of your body as it moves all the way to your head. As it moves, imagine the warmth radiating from the glow of the ring and into your body.

Once the ring reaches your head, imagine it slowly moving down your body, healing as it moves.

Continue to imagine the neon ring slowly moving up and down your body, healing as it does for the remainder of the fifteen minutes.

At the end of the fifteen minutes, do an activity you enjoy or that soothes you. Some activities may be:

- Read a comic
- Exercise
- Sleep
- Watch a superhero movie
- Take a shower
- Talk to someone for support
- Pray
- Cry

Chapter Four: Conquering My Clark Kent façade (Autobiographical)

"You may be able to do things nobody else can do, but that doesn't make it any less hard to be who *you* want to be."

Lana Lang—*Superman: For All Seasons* (1998)

On the blacktop of Woodrow Wilson Elementary School, there was often an in-depth conversation among a large circle of boys on any given weekday. These conversations were always very insightful and packed with knowledge. Often it would begin with a single question, such as: "If you could have one superpower, what would it be?" or "Who would you rather be, Tommy the Green Ranger or Jason the Red Ranger?" Eventually, the conversation would always circle back to the go-to question that is often asked well into adulthood: "Who's your favorite superhero?"

As a middle school teacher, I am asked this question a minimum of once a month. Then and now, I always give the same answer: Superman. The first question would always be followed by "Why?" Without adequate time to provide a response, the questioner would explain how Superman was a cop-out answer because he could not be beaten. Apparently, if he is indestructible, he cannot lose and so cannot be a superhero. Eventually, after having an opportunity to speak, I would simply shrug my shoulders and say, "I don't know. I just like him."

To me, Superman was always better. *Batman: The Animated Series*, *Spider-Man*, *X-Men*, *Iron Man*, and *Justice League* were the shows that occupied the television most mornings as I dressed for school and all afternoons while waiting for my mother to arrive home from K-Mart so I could walk home from Roy and Ms. Della's. But each early Saturday morning, *The New Adventures of Superman* was more highly anticipated. When *Smallville* began to appear on the WB in 2002, I watched each episode religiously, anticipating Clark finally learning to fly or Lana becoming the woman of his dreams. Christopher Reeve helped me understand kindness and generosity as Clark Kent, why I must never kneel before my enemies as Superman, and that if you love a person enough, not even time is an obstacle.

I loved Superman as a kid. When I saw the red cape and emblazoned "S," I never saw the hero. Instead, through my eyes, beneath the "S" curl, I saw Clark Kent and I felt sorry for him, because although Superman always succeeded, Clark Kent never won. He was a nice guy, and he helped me understand why nice guys finish last. Yes, Clark had super abilities that allowed him to fly and smash a Chevy automobile against large boulders, but he never got the girl, friends, or a family of his own. For me, each episode and movie did not show Superman's accomplishments, but the sacrifice of Clark's happiness.

Unlike Batman, who returned to a mansion and a butler after a hard night of fighting crime, when Superman saved the world, he removed his costume, became Clark Kent, and returned to his studio apartment on Clinton Ave. Clark could hear the conversations of people around the world but remained more alone than anyone on the planet. Throughout all of this, Clark never put himself first. He never became bitter, depressed, angry, or anxious. He suffered in silence with a smile, and I loved him for it. Clark helped me understand humility while demonstrating compassion for others who usually deserved no sympathy. Clark Kent helped me believe there is always good in people if you search hard enough. If you smile enough. If you're enough of a good guy.

Because of Clark, I found myself apologizing for mistakes I never made.

Apologizing

I figured out why I say I'm sorry so much. When I was little there were many things that my father didn't do that hurt my mother. He didn't compliment her. He wasn't always nice to her. And he never said he was sorry. But that just didn't apply to my mom. It applied to all of us. My dad never apologized for anything because he thought he did no wrong. Many problems could have been solved if he just said he was sorry. So, I try and make up for the mistakes of my father without even noticing it. So, if someone tells me that I say I'm sorry too much, I'm sorry, it's in my nature, and now you know.

I wrote these words in high school in 2003. At the time, I was living in the basement of my uncle's house with my mother. Our home had been foreclosed by the bank, and me and my mother were homeless. It wasn't the best living situation. The basement would sometimes flood, leaking septic water onto my books, clothes, and sheets. There were also roaches that I could see moving throughout the inside of the Gateway computer I bought with money earned from my paper route, throughout the shower as I washed, and across my bed when I turned on the light to begin the day. All of these things (the foreclosure of our home by the bank, the history of domestic abuse between my parents, their divorce, and my childhood sexual abuse) contributed to a pervasive feeling of being broken, useless, depressed, and trapped in a situation I did not choose. Although I knew this to be true at the time, I quickly realized that complaining about my problems was not an option. Clark taught me that good guys never complain. Instead, they work hard to improve their situation and assist others along the way. Good guys work hard, never ask for help, but are always willing to lend a hand.

It's for this reason I always kept a journal. My safe place. A place where I could vent, explore my thoughts, and not feel judged. I still have these journals and sometimes return to them to remember what I have forgotten (or blocked out). These journals and stories were the only way I could remain sane and view myself as a good guy. At the time, I believed that if I remained a good guy, the world would respond in favor with good karma and a bright future. To do otherwise would make me into a villain—a person who looks out only for himself, cuts corners to get ahead, and steps on the backs of others to achieve success. I believed the only way to be a hero was to suffer in silence and follow the path put forth by Clark Kent.

Apologizing for my mistakes and those of others was the foundation of my childhood that led to the cognitive distortions of *mind reading* and *all-or-nothing thinking* throughout adolescence and into adulthood. I always placed the needs of others before my own. I never set or enforced boundaries. In my mind, this was the difficult-but-worthy path of being a hero. However, unlike Clark, I did not seek happiness. This was not because of a strong moral conscience but because I believed that after being sexually assaulted and raped, I didn't deserve happiness. Depression and sadness was all I was good for. I lived behind the facade of Clark Kent.

Between the late-night shouting matches of my parents, a physical altercation between my brother and father that resulted in a fracture of the family that has yet to heal, and my own sexual abuse at the hands of my older sister, 3027 N. Wilson Dr. became a house filled with consistent inconsistencies, fear, shame, and isolation under the guise of love and affection. In the same way Clark no longer believed he could trust his adopted parents (Jonathan and Marth Kent) to tell the truth following the perpetuated lie of his origins from the moment of his arrival to Earth, I no longer believed I could trust my parents and siblings to look out for my best interest. In the same way Clark also believed the people he loved would eventually abandon him in the same manner as his birth parents, Jor-El and Lara, I believed others would eventually let me down, leaving me alone and worse off than before, and so the only one I could depend on was myself.

At the time, I identified as both a *lost child* and as a *family hero*. To not suffer wrath from the adults who could dictate my happiness, I developed the superpower of invisibility by blending into my surroundings. Rather than draw attention to myself or be forced to interact with others, I performed activities requiring isolation and independence, such as reading, distance running, speech, debate, and drama. To establish a sense of financial security, I delivered newspapers for the *Peoria Journal Star* in the morning and flipped burgers at the fast food restaurant, Velvet Freeze, located across the street, and set up chairs and stands for the rehearsals and concerts of the Peoria Symphony Orchestra. These jobs not only paid for my school supplies and clothes, but graduation packet, ACT testing, and college admission fees. Remaining busy and silent was the only way I knew to conceal my beliefs of being different and feeling like an outsider.

Adults often described me as an old soul who was responsible and had it all together. Admiration of teachers and coaches, along with the accolades that came from cross country, speech, drama, and academics lessened (but did not eliminate) feelings of inadequacy and shame. The positive praise of adults made me feel less worthless, so I became a people pleaser and a fixer of problems for those who seemed unable to manage the difficulties of life. At the time, the inconvenience and pressure of feeling the need to be dependable was nothing compared to the shame and filth I saw in the mirror if I didn't meet my expectations.

By the time I reached college at Bowling Green State University in Ohio, the Clark Kent facade had established permanent residence in my psyche. Setting boundaries was an impossibility if I was going to be liked and accepted by others. On the surface, I was happy. Around friends I became the life of any gathering with jokes and off-the-wall shenanigans that made others laugh and feel comfortable. Behind closed doors, I would sometimes spend entire days curled in the fetal position in the center of my bed feeling empty, unmotivated, and wishing someone would save me. I was left waiting for my Superman, which I believed I had found in my wife, Sarah.

Marriage, career, and a stable home brought relief, but it did not bring happiness or relieve anxiety. I still lived in a state of perpetual fear and hypervigilance, waiting and planning for the next tragedy, or for the people I loved to unexpectedly leave without warning or reason. Personal boundaries were nonexistent. I continued to wait for someone to take away my pain and make me feel complete.

"Yes," "okay," "I can fix that," "I'm fine," and "I'm sorry" were phrases that filled my day from morning to night, but without the same calming effects that people pleasing produced in the past. Fawning no longer provided me a sense of comfort and happiness. Instead, I developed a sense of resentment for others who were making *me* be the source of *their* happiness. I viewed myself as the victim being stripped of their time, money, and sense of well-being for the sake of others. My wife, children, friends, coworkers, and students had become the enemies of my happiness rather than the source of my joy. I often thought, "If I can make them happy, why can't they do the same for me? It isn't fair." In my mind, they were being abusive and manipulative, when in fact they were just being human. They had no idea I was hurting because I never told them. I never let them see behind the facade. As *protection,* I cut myself off from social interaction. I became numb, lifeless. I became the villain, until I made the choice to begin recovering from the traumas of my past and developing the ability to set appropriate boundaries to ensure my own physical, spiritual, emotional, and mental well-being.

In the beginning, I worked with my therapist, Susan, learning how to set appropriate boundaries and feel safe in my own skin. I remember Susan telling me that I had to spend fifteen minutes a day meditating in my safe place as part of my path toward recovery. Fifteen minutes in a safe place of my own creation. Fifteen minutes of breathing, soothing sounds, relaxation, and reflection. At the time, it was fifteen minutes of hell!

Over the course of four years, those fifteen minutes of meditation became moments in the day I would look forward to. They would bring the peace of mind, calmness, and forgiveness I had never known when attempting to please the people around me and keep my mind busy with an overabundance of tasks. Eventually, I no longer needed to meditate in my safe place. I felt secure and safe enough in my body to meditate in my bedroom with headphones or in my classroom during my planning period. Those fifteen minutes helped me learn how to set appropriate boundaries and begin conquering my Clark Kent facade.

Setting Appropriate Boundaries

The most difficult part of conquering the Clark Kent facade is maintaining boundaries. It's easy to fall into old habits when pushed by individuals who may have a problem with you setting boundaries for yourself and them. I found this most difficult with my father. A number of years ago, when I first began my journey of recovery, I told my father that I had been raped by my sister (his daughter) for two years when I was eight to ten. After explaining the details of the sexual abuse, assault, and rape, he told me, "Forget about it. It's in the past. The best thing you can do is move on." Rather than cower and continue to harbor the secret I had been carrying for over twenty years, I responded with defiance and honesty. I told him that I couldn't forget. The abuse was something I had to live with every day and that it could not be forgotten.

He apologized, hung up, and did not speak with me for nine months. It was not until my brother Daniel told him that he needed to start talking to me that my father proceeded to text and talk with me as if nothing had occurred. As if I had not told him about my sexual abuse. The illusion of normalcy was not something I could return to. So, after speaking with Susan, we established the boundary that in order for me and my father to continue having a relationship, my father would have to write a letter in which he apologized for abandoning me after I told him about my sexual assault. I told this to my father. He responded via text and said:

Okay, son. I will respect your request. You are a grown man and able to make your own decisions. I'm glad you are doing better and I'm really sorry to hear about Sarah's brother. Let me say this: I love my kids the same. You, Daniel, and (my sister) are my life. I don't love one more or less than the other one. If I could take your hurt, I would. I can't, so I can do only what I am able to do. But remember this. We can only start healing after we forgive. If I could change things, I would. I'm sure your sister is hurting. I'm sure she had no intention of hurting you. Then or now. She has to live with the fact of what she did and face everyone who read your book and label her a rapist. This has to be really hard for her. I'm sure this has been really hard on you. I can only imagine how hard it has been. I know my kid and I know you are strong. You can and will overcome this. It's in the blood. No matter what you think, this too will pass. If you need me, I will always be there for you. Don't be a stranger. I don't want you to one day think I missed out on a lot of my family's life. She, Daniel, Tina, and me are your family. Love you unconditionally. Da

In *Heroes, Villains, and Healing,* I analyzed what this message meant, the impact it had on me then, and the possible thoughts my father had after writing it. I explain how the message minimized my sexual abuse and sympathized with my abuser (my sister) rather than myself (the survivor) when he wrote, "She has to live with the fact of what she did and face everyone who read your book and label her a rapist." His words reveal the need to not "air dirty laundry" (regarded as a major taboo among the black community) and hold others accountable for their actions when using correct language to describe an abuser's behavior. It is regrettable to have to use this word when referring to my sister, but to do otherwise would mean not holding her accountable for her actions and perpetuating my need to hide behind the mask of the Clark Kent facade.

Second, the message reveals my father's refusal to take responsibility for his failure as a parent to protect his children. Although he writes, "If I could take your hurt I would," this statement (and others) do not reveal his knowledge or acceptance of his role in allowing my sexual abuse to occur. A parent's responsibility is to protect their children. To not do so does not mean the parent has failed in their parental duties, because there is no such thing as a perfect parent. Mistakes will be made. However, following those mistakes, parents must admit their shortcomings to let their children know what occurred was not their fault and for the parent to apply what they have learned to future situations. Unfortunately, my father did not accept any accountability for his actions and so placed the blame of my sexual abuse on the shoulders of others, including myself.

Finally, it reveals the mentality of many men, especially black men who came of age before and during the Civil Rights Movement. My father writes statements such as, "I know my kid and I know you are strong," and, "It's in the blood." His statements reveal a need to teach boys to remain silent, emotionless, numb, and move on after life's hardships without healing or acknowledging that they took place. For older black men this is especially true because during the civil rights movement and the era of Jim Crow throughout the Deep South, denial of pain, hardship, and abuse was the only way to survive. It was a commonly used coping mechanism to handle physical abuse and the mental trauma of not being able to keep their family safe. Denial of having been hurt could have prevented men like my father from being lynched and killed as he grew up in rural Mississippi. Denial and forgetting were the only coping strategies fathers could pass on to their sons when basic human rights had been stripped away. This means that when their sons, nephews, and cousins suffered a traumatic episode (such as childhood sexual abuse), they would teach and reinforce the only way of life they had known by forgetting it ever happened and burying the emotions that accompany trauma. This does not justify his response to my sexual abuse, but it provides context. As a male survivor, it means no longer viewing myself as a victim, understanding the wrongs of the past, learning from them, and moving forward to conquer my facade.

In the summer of 2018, while writing and publishing the self-help guide *How to Kill Your Batman*, I had yet to receive a letter of apology, so my father and I had no communication. In August of that same summer, Daniel (my brother) called to inform me that my father was having serious medical problems and not managing his diabetes. Photos of my father's legs forced me to call in an attempt to tell him to stop being stubborn and go to the hospital.

When I called my father, I lied and told him that I had called an ambulance to take him to the hospital, but he still refused. After he made a series of excuses about not having the money to make an appointment with the VA hospital, I became angry. Really angry! My father's pride and stubbornness pushed me over the edge.

I began cursing and telling him how he had not prepared me for how hard life could be. Through tears, I told him how my wife and I had almost gone bankrupt attempting to survive paying for daycare and attempting to survive on the salary of two teachers. How fear of losing our house in Baltimore the same way I had last my home in Peoria due to his irresponsibility made me stubborn, just like him. To survive, we sold our home and moved to Ohio to be closer to family and keep our heads above water. I explained how we were living with my in-laws and attempted, to the best of my ability, to articulate my anxiety, fear, and feelings of failure as a father and husband.

I yelled.

I screamed.

I begged for an answer.

Why would he not apologize for leaving me when I needed him the most? His response: "I can't do something I don't believe is right."

My world stopped.

Until that moment, I believed, beyond a doubt, that my father did not understand what I wanted from him to begin to repair our broken relationship. I thought that maybe he believed the text message he sent constituted an apology. His response proved that I was being naive.

There were no more tears as I heard him say, "It's good to hear your voice."

There was no more emotion as I heard him ask, "How are my grandbabies doing?"

I believed I had lost my father.

Afterward, I told him to take care of himself and ended the phone call.

In the home of my mother and father-in-law, after selling my home and ending the career and life I had made with my wife and children, I cried. I mourned the loss of my father. I mourned the loss of my childhood. I mourned the loss of my family of origin.

I had never felt so alone and such a failure.

Maintaining Boundaries

As a boy, I remember my mother telling me a story that filled me with terror, remorse, and sadness. The story involved a young boy my age, a mother, a wooden post, a hammer, and a box of nails. I do not know how old I was at the time she told me the tale, but I am thirty-four years old now, and I can still see the layout of our kitchen and the sober expression of exhaustion on my mother's face. The story has remained anchored in my memory all these years mostly because my mother is not a storyteller. Her primary role has always been caregiver to her children and her ten younger siblings.

I sat at the kitchen table as she stood near the stove and began to speak.

She said there was once a little boy who was always very mean to his mother. Rather than say thank you and I love you, he would yell at her, call her names, and treat her like garbage. One day, after the little boy said another mean comment to his mother, she stopped what she was doing, calmly took a hammer and nail outside to a wooden fence post, and hammered the nail into the wood. Afterward, she returned to the house, put the hammer away, and continued with the day as if nothing out of the ordinary had taken place. The young boy was confused but said nothing.

The next day it happened again. Following his rude and disrespectful comment to her, she took a hammer and nail outside to the fence post, hammered the nail into the wood of the post, returned to the house, and continued with the day. Her actions seemed odd, but still the boy did not ask her to explain.

The routine continued day in and day out. The boy would say or do something rude and disrespectful. Afterward, his mother would hammer a nail into the post and continue with the day. Finally, one day the young boy asked his mother, "Why are you hammering nails into the fence post outside?"

The mother responded, "They are a reminder."

"A reminder of what?" asked the young boy.

"A reminder of how often you treat me rudely and with disrespect," she said.

The boy became quiet. Curious, the boy ventured to the fence post. Staring in shock and confusion, he saw that it was littered with so many nails that some had become bent, warped, and turned in on one another. Seeing this, the young boy felt ashamed and knew he had treated his mother poorly.

Realizing the error of his ways, he tried to set things right. He began treating his mother kindly. He helped with the chores throughout the house, gave her compliments, and treated her with respect. With each kind act and words of praise, the mother returned to the fence post and removed a nail. It took time, but eventually each nail was removed. When this day arrived, the mother asked her son to join her outside. Once outside, the mother took her son to the post and asked him what he saw.

The young boy said with a smile, "All the nails are gone. Aren't you happy, Mother?"

Without a smile, the mother looked at her son and asked, "What else do you see?"

The young boy did not know what to say. He saw nothing.

While staring at the post, the mother said, "Yes, my son. All the nails are gone, but look at the wood. The nails have been removed, but the scars they created are still there. Those won't go away easily."

When the story came to an end, I felt a mixture of emotions as I thought about the young boy and how there was nothing he could do to heal the scars he had inflicted on his mother. I was also confused and concerned. Was there something I had done to my mother that I could not take back? The story has stuck with me all these years and came to my mind when my father finally apologized for telling me, in September of 2019, to forget that my sexual abuse had ever occurred. Rather than write a letter, as requested, my father sent a text message in which he said:

Sorry, son, that I wasn't there for you when you really needed me. I didn't know. I will give my life for you. You, Daniel, and (my sister) was and are my life. I apologize. I love and miss you.

I accepted the apology.

It was not a handwritten letter as originally requested, but it was an apology, and it was all that I had asked for. I remained firm but also pliable in my boundaries, and my request had been fulfilled.

His act of kindness allowed me to remove a nail from the post in the same manner as the mother and the disrespectful son. However, although the nail had been removed, and the apology had been made, the scar remained. Apologizing was enough to remove one nail from the post, but what about the other nails? What about the numerous other scars? More than a text message apology was needed to heal the scars, to remove the other nails that had been hammered in over the years, to rebuild our broken relationship.

Today, I do keep in contact with my father. We do not speak every day, or even text every week. We communicate when we must, if at all. I know it will take time and work to heal the scars he created. We both must reestablish a relationship with the other in order to know the man I have become after years of therapy and recovery. Conquering my Clark Kent facade and establishing consistent boundaries created a new identity that has become complete and more stable than the facade of the past. My new identity is loving, kind, and generous, but strong enough to distance me from those who could hinder my growth or damage my family of choice. In place of the Clark Kent facade stands more than a survivor. In its place is an overcomer.

PART TWO:
THE SUPERMAN FACADE

"A job as a reporter on a big newspaper will keep me in touch with those who may need my help! I'll wear glasses, pretend to be timid, but when I'm needed I'll wear this costume and the world will know of Superman!"

Superman—*Superman* #53 (1948), "The Origin of Superman"

In *Superman* #149 (1961), "The Death of Superman: Part One," Jerry Siegel presents readers with an alternate reality in which Lex Luthor is no longer a minion of evil. Instead, he decides to live a life of good deeds while staying on the straight and narrow. In the first few pages of the comic, Lex repents his life of crime, deciding to use his intelligence to help humanity prosper rather than impair its growth in his attempts to kill Superman. To demonstrate his reformation, he creates a cure for cancer and is granted parole after Superman vouches for the former criminal.

Later, in "The Death of Superman: Part Two," Lex's newfound good nature is not well received among the criminals of Metropolis. Angry at Lex's renunciation of his life of crime, thugs and gangsters who used to praise the criminal attempt to take his life. In fact, so many attempts are made on Lex's life that Superman decides to build the former villain a space station laboratory to ensure the scientist's safety as he works to solve the ailments of humanity.

After a week of isolation, Lex sends out a distress beacon. Superman quickly responds to the SOS. Once inside the satellite, Superman realizes it is a trap, as Lex bombards the hero with green kryptonite. Weakened and caught off guard, Lex straps the Man of Steel to a surgical table with kryptonite straps and beams down intense doses of kryptonite radiation from above. As an extra layer of cruelty, Lex forces Lois Lane, Jimmy Olsen, and Perry White to watch as their friend and hero dies a slow, agonizing death. On the brink of death and barely conscious, Lex tells Superman:

> I discovered that cancer cure in order to be released from jail. I pretended to have reformed so I could lull you into a false sense of security! The purpose, to catch you off guard and lure you into this death trap! Those gangland attempts against my life were on the level! The underworld didn't suspect I was playing a cunning role! How they hated me! But they'll feel differently about me now, eh?

It is then that Superman takes his final breath and dies. With green-tinted skin and a costume absent of color, Superman lays still and lifeless. Lex lifts his arms in triumphant success as Lois, Jimmy, and Perry shed tears for the fallen hero.

In this comic, Jerry Siegel creates a story in which Lex Luthor defeats the Man of Steel, not because Lex is stronger, faster, or smarter than Superman. It is not even because Lex outsmarts the Big Blue Boy Scout. Instead, Superman is defeated because he is too trusting. Siegel creates a reality in which Superman lets his guard down too easily when he should have remained vigilant against his archnemesis.

While the story appears far-fetched in its 60s style, dialogue, and drawings, the comic helps provide a context for understanding why male survivors of childhood sexual abuse may be afraid to allow themselves to be vulnerable and intimate with friends, family, and loved ones. Similar to the way Lex Luthor betrays Superman when the hero least expects it, many male survivors fear they will be betrayed in the same manner when they are at their most vulnerable.

For male survivors, trusting others means relinquishing power and putting it in the hands of those who can do the most harm while hiding behind a supposed guise of friendship. Fear of being betrayed makes many male survivors guard their emotions. Unfortunately, these fears create a self-fulfilling prophecy of distrust in relationships, leading to isolation, loneliness, shame, and guilt. Although these fears may by justified for a child in need of safety, for an adult it has the potential to transform the hero of any story into a villain.

This part of *How to Conquer Your Inner Superman* helps male survivors of childhood sexual abuse understand why the Superman facade is used as a coping mechanism to the trauma of being sexually abused. This part also explores the formation of "the hero code," the consequences of maintaining the Superman facade into adulthood, and the tools needed to conquer the Superman facade to become more than a hero or a villain, but a survivor and overcomer.

Chapter Five: Understanding the Superman Facade

"It feels good to help people."

Clark Kent—*Superman: American Alien* (2016)

Comic books that have the most developed characters (whether Superman, Batman, or any other superhero) are those that tell the story of a hero at their beginning as they learn and grow from their mistakes. Unlike origin stories, these comics delve into the alter ego of the hero, exploring who they are and what they stand for while attempting to cope with their newfound superhuman abilities. The hero searches to find direction, knowing they can no longer save the day as themselves. They know they must become more than a person, they must become a symbol, an idea. What truly makes these comics impressive is that the reader gets a glimpse of a hero's humanity as they shape and mold their hero code into existence. *Superman: American Alien* (2016), "Eagle" by Mark Landis best illustrates this metamorphosis of Superman.

In this comic, Clark Kent is not a child learning to understand and develop his superhuman abilities. Instead, he is a young adult attempting to find his place as a journalist and potential hero. In essence, he is learning the ropes through trial and a lot of error. He barely resembles the Superman fans have grown to know and love throughout his eighty years of existence. Rather than the usual form-fitting costume of red, blue, and gold, this young Superman in training wears jeans, knee pads, combat boots, an aviator's helmet with goggles, black cape (ripped from Batman's face in a previous issue), a black tee-shirt, and a bulletproof vest sporting the classic Superman "S" spray-painted white.

Here, Superman as a symbol of hope begins to take shape. The beginning of this metamorphosis is demonstrated in a phone conversation between Clark and his mother, Martha Kent, while in Metropolis. He tells her:

> I try to do one good deed a day. I use a police radio. I just do what I can. I'm only an intern at the *Planet*, and I take my own lunches, so no one notices. It's not hurting my social life. I'm fine—No, I haven't gone out at night, I have a full-time job. It feels good to help people.

Here, Superman lacks the confidence he will eventually develop, demonstrating that nothing worth achieving happens overnight, whether it is the development of Clark Kent into Superman or the creation of the Superman facade by male survivors. This chapter explains the birth of the male survivor's Superman facade and how and why this separate identity develops following the trauma of childhood sexual abuse.

The Superman Facade and Childhood Sexual Abuse

When you read the name Superman, what image comes to mind?

When you hear "Man of Steel," do you visualize a large red "S" emblazoned on a background of gold in the center of the superhero's chest with a matching, perfectly curled "S" dangling from his jet-black hair?

How do you feel when you hear the phrase, "Look up in the sky! It's a bird! It's a plane! No, it's Superman!"? Are you filled with hope and confidence that the day will be saved?

You may picture bullets bouncing off the chest of the hero as he swoops in, foils the bad guy's plan for world domination, and flies away with a smile, never asking for a thank-you in return. You may be filled with a sense of unwavering optimism in believing, beyond the shadow a doubt, that everything will work out fine and good will triumph over evil.

For this reason, Superman is more than the first superhero; he is the best. He does what is right rather than what is easy, no matter how difficult the choice may be. He is a savior and a true hero who is always willing to sacrifice himself to save a single human life. He is strong, kind, confident, and unbeatable. In essence, he is perfect! With these qualities, it makes sense why children double knot bath towels around their neck and run through their home with fists in the air pretending to be the Man of Steel.

Being Superman feels good. It feels right. Being Superman and possessing his abilities to run faster than a speeding bullet and leap buildings in a single bound is everything a survivor wishes they could be and do. This is because, rather than feeling strong and confident like Superman, male survivors of child sexual abuse live in a constant state of fear, anxiety, stress, and worry. Ellen Bass explains in *The Courage to Heal* how many male survivors who have been sexually abused as children tend to feel:

- Bad, dirty, or ashamed
- Different from other people
- That there's something wrong deep down inside
- That if people really knew them, they'd leave
- A pervasive sense of shame
- Alienated or isolated

These feelings cause some survivors to:

- Hate themselves
- Feel compelled to be perfect

These emotions and thoughts are the exact opposite of what it means to be Superman. It's why male survivors sometimes cope with the effects of these negative thoughts and feelings by creating a Superman facade to fake being confident and in control.

The Superman facade is born to filter the thoughts, feelings, beliefs, and behaviors that survivors feel about themselves through the lens of a savior in order to feel safe through predictability. Some survivors of childhood sexual abuse create a Superman facade because during early development they live in a constant state of unpredictability and fear. This is a time when a child needs consistency and routine to develop confidence in themselves. This is when children build positive and secure relationships with caregivers and other adults. But children who are sexually abused do not, and often cannot, create secure attachments to adults and other individuals. They lose the skills needed to create a positive view of the world. To cope, some latch onto the predictability and safety of superheroes, adopting the behavior of heroes to develop a Superman facade that lives by a hero code of their own creation.

Male survivors of childhood sexual abuse live in chaos filled with fear, shame, and guilt from their sexual abuse and from unreliable adults who are unable to provide protection and safety. However, in the world of superheroes and comics, whether on television or on art-filled pages, heroes provide the predictability of safety. They follow a code of doing what is right and punishing the bad guys, a code they wish adults possessed in reality. No matter if a superhero has the ability to fly, move at lightning speed, or materialize objects with the help of a super-charged ring, each hero shares a code to protect the weak and a consistency of doing what is right, which is what the children survivors need.

The hero code is an unwritten code that guides a hero's actions, separating their behavior from that of a villain, informing the survivor how not to become like their abuser, creating a definition of safety that is not provided by caregivers. The hero code defines the core of a superhero's character while also dictating the rules need to function under the guise of a Superman facade. Without the hero code, both the hero and the survivor would be lost.

The male survivor who develops a Superman facade develops a black-and-white view of the world, filled with absolute beliefs of right and wrong. These young males latch on to the rules of their hero code for safety and predictability, but mostly because of the benefits associated with helping others while maintaining a sense of control. Seth J. Gillihan, PhD, explains in *Cognitive Behavior Therapy Made Simple* how helping others leads to improvements in anxiety and depression symptoms. He states how researchers have found that:

- Focusing on others can distract from one's own distress.
- Helping others provides a sense of meaning and purpose.
- Prosocial behaviors may cause the release of oxytocin, which is involved in trust and bonding with others.
- Doing nice things may stimulate the release of dopamine.
- Reaching out to others may lower activity in the stress response system.

Meaning the Superman facade is an attempt for the survivor to:

- Be liked and accepted by others in an attempt to eliminate feelings of isolation,
- Ensure the survivor does not identify with their abuser in an attempt to not become a villain,
- Latch on to predictable and positive examples of caregivers,
- Hide their feelings of shame and guilt with smiles and kindness to eliminate feelings of shame and self-hatred.

To illustrate how the Superman facade can translate into a hero code male survivors feel obligated to follow, there is no better comic to be used than *Actions Comics #775.*

Superman's Hero Code

Believing in and living by a hero code is the foundation of the Superman facade for male survivors of childhood sexual abuse. The best example that can be used to understand the hero code of Superman, how it dictates his actions, and how male survivors develop and live by their own hero code is *Action Comics #775* (2001), "What's So Funny About Truth, Justice, and the American Way?"

In this epic comic, Superman is forced to confront his ethical belief to never, under any circumstances, kill when he meets a team of superheroes known as the Elite. These antiheroes live by a different hero code. These four individuals, led by Manchester Black (a telekinetic with purple hair, a black trench coat, and a shirt decorated with the British Flag), have no problem killing the villains they defeat in an attempt to rid the world of crime, once and for all, and send a message to other villains that crime will no longer be tolerated. The difference between the hero code of the Elite and Superman can be seen in a conversation the first time Black and Superman meet face-to-face.

Superman, while angry, grabs Manchester by the arm and tells him he can't murder people if he is going to call himself a hero. Black responds:

> You may not believe this, but as a kid, I used to love "heroes," though I never used the word for us. Good pounding the snot out of evil in bright tights. No questions. No "grey areas." It was a perfect bloody dream for a boy who lost a mother to lung cancer an' a father to Adolf. An' then I woke up. Masks are for hiding, capes are for play. "Villains" don't share their plans before they smoke you—'cept in campaign speeches, or the pulpit, or in front of the classroom. Reality is a mite bloodier than sitcoms. The greys stretch out farther.

Before being teleported from their ship, Superman tells Black, "I'm not an idiot, Black, I know there are bad men in power and the world is not an equitable place—but you can't throw morality in the garbage just because life's tough!"

Eventually, the comic comes to end with a battle of the opposing codes. Black, now seeing Superman as a threat, uses the Elite to try and kill the Man of Steel. Believing they have won, Superman turns the tables. He kills each member of the Elite, one by one—at least that's what everyone believes. Using his super abilities, Superman makes it appear he has killed all of them, when in actuality he has knocked them all unconscious and given Black a concussion to prevent the villain from losing his powers. Believing Superman lobotomized him using his heat vision, he looks into the cameras broadcasting the battle with tears streaming from his eyes:

> You c-can't do this! You . . . You're Superman . . . You don't . . . you don't do this. You . . . They saw! Everyone on Earth saw, you degenerate! Everyone saw what you did to us and they know! They know you're no better than us! You're no better! There's nothing special about you!

With a smile, Superman tells Black and the rest of the world:

> Yes . . . they did see, didn't they? They saw all the ugliness. The anger . . . and I bet it frightened them. It frightened me. When I decided to cross the line . . . do what you do . . . I was terrified. Thought it would be tough. But you know what? Anger is easy. Vengeance and spite are easy. Lucky for you . . . and for me . . . I don't like my heroes ugly and mean. Just don't believe in it.

The comic ends with Superman telling Black, "Dreams save us. Dreams lift us up and transform us. And on my soul, I swear . . . until my dream of a world where dignity, honor, and justice becomes the reality we all share, I'll never stop fighting. Ever." These last few words reveal the true hero code of Superman to never stop fighting for the world he believes in. The foundations of this hero code were established as a child, in Smallville, Kansas, as Clark Kent and can be seen in the four-part comic *Superman: For All Seasons* (1998) by Tim Sale and Jeff Loeb.

Birth of the Superman Facade

Each part of *Superman: For All Seasons* is titled a different season. The first season in the comic is spring, and in this part Superman does not exist. There is only Clark Kent. Although his abilities have fully developed, making him the strongest being on Earth, he still feels worthless. He does not feel normal. Tim Sale does an excellent job of portraying the feelings of loneliness and isolation as he walks with Lana after dinner, lies in bed listening to his parents talk about him on the front porch, and standing alone in the middle of a field after outrunning a train. It is not until a tornado touches down in Smallville that Clark's feelings of having no self-worth begin to fade.

As Clark is swept up into a tornado and pieces of his shirt are ripped from beneath his overalls, he says, "I can handle this. I know I can." In that moment, Clark learns to fly and saves the life of a gas station attendant as gasoline ignites, causing an explosion. When the storm passes and a large portion of the town is destroyed, Clark returns home. With a tractor over his head while hovering in midair, Clark tells his parents, "You should see what it looks like in town. I can't help thinking—I could have done more."

Afterward, Clark decides to leave Smallville, go to Metropolis, and become Superman in an attempt to do good. To save people. To be a hero. When this decision is made, the facade of Superman takes shape as he becomes Metropolis's personal superhero.

What is important to know is that although being a help to others can feel good, it does not eliminate underlying thoughts of being different and living a life that seems alien. This is evident in Clark's conversation with his mother, Martha, about becoming Superman. He tells her while sitting on the porch swing of their country home, looking up at the stars, "It's just—even with all the good I've done? Sometimes I seem out of place in the city. And I always thought Smallville would feel like home. Now, it's different here, too." Clark's continued sense of loneliness and isolation as

Superman is because being a savior and helping others can only provide so much comfort for a short period of time. Soon the feeling fades away, and the person beneath the facade is all that is left. If healing does not take place, perfectionism of the facade will feel like the only option toward feeling and being normal.

Clark learning to perfect his Superman facade can be seen in parts two and three of *Superman: For All Seasons*, "Summer" and "Fall." Throughout each part, as he saves Metropolis from being impacted by a submarine missile, rescuing a scientist from a chemical fire at Chemo Labs, and putting Lex Luthor behind bars (for a night), Superman becomes more confident in his abilities to always be there to save the day. With each success, Superman's facade solidifies Superman's hero code.

As the facade of Superman becomes more defined, there comes the need to save everyone and accomplish all tasks (no matter how difficult, complicated, or numerous) perfectly and alone. Perfectionism also creates the belief that with more success comes the pressure of failure. The Superman facade means believing there is a need to always be there in time, always getting the perfect score, always being the best, and always overcoming all obstacles to exceed expectations. To fall short, even once or by a small margin, would mean failure, allowing feelings of shame to return, along with more severe feelings of isolation and loneliness.

Birth of Your Superman Facade

As a result of your childhood sexual abuse, you may have developed a rigid style of interpersonal effectiveness to combat feelings of shame. A rigid style of interpersonal effectiveness means tending to withdraw from relationships and believing you are safest and most powerful when working alone and being alone. This creates a schema reinforced by negative beliefs that you must always have to take care of tasks yourself because responsibilities cannot be trusted to be completed correctly by others.

As a child, following the trauma of sexual abuse, a rigid interpersonal personality in the form of a Superman facade may have saved you from harm, allowing you to survive and possibly even to thrive. Over time, the Superman facade may have created the belief that your childhood sexual abuse gave you superpowers similar to those of Superman, to accomplish tasks with precision and perfection others could not. While your childhood sexual abuse may have developed a means of hyperarousal similar to Superman's heightened sense and ability, maintaining this view of yourself and your actions into adulthood has the potential to create resentment for believing you must always take care of and provide for others. Similar to Superman, you may attempt to protect others who you view as weaker than yourself while attempting to also stay in control.

Both you and Superman attempt to protect and take care of others while hiding feelings of shame and guilt. According to **Internal Family Systems (IFS) Therapy**, these thoughts associated with the Superman facade create a damaged ego that attempts to heal itself in the form of a manager. Like Superman, the manager attempts to protect you, the survivor, from vulnerable feelings of guilt, shame, and low self-esteem by trying to remain in control of any and all situations. Staying in control means maintaining a tight grip on the power that was stripped away after being sexually abused. Unfortunately, there are consequences to maintaining a rigid style of interpersonal effectiveness into adulthood that can transform even a superhero such as Superman into a villain.

Chapter Six: Consequences of the Superman Facade

"Why don't you just put the whole world in a bottle, Superman?"

Lex Luthor—*Superman: Red Son* (2014)

In *Superman #247* "Must There Be a Superman?" (1972), Superman has a conversation with the Guardians (a race of immortals who survey and safeguard the galaxy and who created the Green Lantern Corps) in which they make Superman question his actions as a hero of Earth. These ancient beings walk a fine line in attempting to only observe and not to interfere in a species' development, while also attempting to police the galaxy with the help of the Green Lantern Corps. In this issue, the Guardians help to heal Superman's injuries after saving the universe from intergalactic spores. When Superman awakes, the Guardians tell him that he is interfering with the social growth of humans. The hint that his actions are doing more harm than good is slight, but it is enough to force Superman to question his role as a hero. He begins to wonder if he is becoming a superpowered "big brother," forcing others to depend on him too much and too often instead of becoming more self-reliant.

Upon returning to Earth, Superman is faced with a moral and ethical dilemma. While traveling over America, Superman witnesses a young boy being beaten by his boss while working in an orange field. Superman lands. With his arrival, the other workers, who were silent when the young boy was being beaten, stand angry and yelling for Superman to seek vengeance. Instead, Superman takes pause and remembers his conversation with the Guardians. He takes the young boy home, where the workers ask Superman to build them new homes, improve their working conditions, and put their boss, Senor Harley, in jail for employee maltreatment. Surrounded, and with the words of the Guardians echoing throughout his thoughts, Superman tells the people, "Whatever help you claim you need must come from yourselves." As if by a twist of fate, an earthquake strikes the area, and the homes of the workers collapse to the ground. Now conflicted, Superman decides to rebuild their houses. Pleased with their new homes, Superman tells them:

> Let's get something straight! Sure, I rebuilt your homes, but that was because an earthquake is something you can't handle, something you can't safeguard yourselves against. But you must not count on Superman to patch up your lives every time you have a crisis or disaster. You don't need a Superman! What you really need is a super-will to be guardians of your own identity.

This comic helps to demonstrate one of the problems with perfectionism that will be discussed and explored throughout this chapter. The words of the Guardians and those of Superman pertain to the difference between perfectionism and growth. While a person living behind the facade of Superman can seek perfectionism, eventually it will grow to encompass all parts and people in the life of a survivor. The need for perfectionism causes some survivors to attempt to maintain control of a situation or project in hopes of feeling safe. Unfortunately, the control of perfectionism limits the growth and potential of others.

This chapter addresses and explains why the Superman facade hurts not only male survivors, but those closest to them as well, controlling the nuances of a workplace, families of choice, and the intimate relationships built with others.

The Superman Facade and Perfectionism

One of the most admirable traits of Superman (and possibly why so many male survivors idolize the hero) is his belief that he can save everyone and accomplish all tasks perfectly because of his superpowered abilities. This belief in being able to accomplish all tasks alone without any flaws is *perfectionism*. The Superman facade of male survivors is fueled by the need for perfectionism because of perpetuated feelings of shame stemming from the trauma of being sexually abused as a child.

Arielle Schwartz, PhD, explains in *The Complex PTSD Workbook* that shame is the belief that *you*, not your actions, are bad. Some thoughts that perpetuate shame are:

- "There must be something wrong with me!"
- "I'm so stupid."
- "I can't seem to do anything right."
- "I'm an emotional wreck."
- "I'm just lazy."

Mary Beth Williams, PhD, LCSW, CTS, and Solili Poijula, PhD, go on to explain in *The PTSD Workbook* that shame goes beyond guilt and is more difficult to overcome. While guilt means feeling bad for what you may or may not have done during a traumatic event, shame means feeling bad for who you are.

Many male survivors feel shame for being a sexual abuse survivor because of societal assumptions that boys and men cannot be sexually abused or assaulted. In an attempt to alleviate feelings of shame, they develop the belief that only perfection is acceptable. This has the potential to create a shame-based identity, according to Babette Rothschild. The perfectionism created by the Superman facade is developed to cope with feelings of inadequacy, inferiority, and embarrassment of being a male survivor. With the Superman facade of perfectionism, adult male survivors attempt to hide feelings of low self-worth by accumulating accolades and by reaching physical or monetary perfection. This lets them appear confident and act as if they have it all together.

You may be wondering, after reading *How to Kill Your Batman*, how hypervigilance is different from perfectionism. In the same way Superman and Batman are similar in their goals and approaches to ensure justice as superheroes, perfectionism and hypervigilance are similar but not identical.

Perfectionism vs. Hypervigilance

Perfectionism and hypervigilance are very similar coping mechanisms, and each is embodied by two of Earth's mightiest heroes: Superman and Batman. Because of the similarity between the two coping strategies, the two heroes get along well (some of the time) and work well together (most of the time), while also clashing in matters of opinion about how to administer justice. The best example that differentiates the two characters and their coping strategies can be seen in the graphic novel *Kingdom Come* (1996) by Mark Waid and Alex Ross.

Kingdom Come is set in a future where both Superman and Batman have grown old. To ensure justice and order is maintained throughout the twenty-first century, Superman takes it on himself to regulate the actions of other metahumans gifted with superhuman abilities to limit the number of human casualties. As Superman prepares to come out of retirement, he asks Bruce Wayne to join his new Justice League, but the Dark Knight refuses. While in the Batcave, Batman tells Superman:

> Frictions have been building to a head for years, Clark. The metahuman population boomed while you were gone, and once ordinary folks decided you and I were too gentle and old-fashioned to face the challenges of the twenty-first century. They wanted their "heroes" stronger and more ruthless. Be careful what you wish for. Right now, the metahumans have the keys to Earth's kingdom. Wrestling control is a delicate matter. It requires finesse and meticulous, careful planning against those enemies more hidden, but it can be done. Without, I might add, Superman and the Justice League booming into town—punching now, asking questions later . . . I have my own controls in place, thank you. They may be slower and more methodical than yours,

but they get results. You used to brag that Metropolis was a utopia next to Gotham. Now who has the utopia?

Superman responds:

Some paradise. From what I can see, Gotham is nearly a police state. You always favored scaring people into obeying the law, but this. You're willing to turn ordinary citizens into a superstitious and cowardly lot?

Both characters' words to the other reveal the flaws in each other's ability to administer justice. Superman, while having the ability to be hypersensitive, uses brute force to make others abide by his rules. Batman demonstrates this when he says, "The Justice League booming into town—punching now and asking questions later." This is the power of perfectionism. It may not always be right, but it is right to the person seeking to ensure perfectionism, meaning "it's either my way or the highway." While this may also be true for hypervigilance, perfectionism uses more force to *make* the pieces fit, rather than matching and fitting the pieces together with precision. Batman demonstrates this difference when he tells Superman, "It requires finesse and meticulous, careful planning against those enemies more hidden."

Hypervigilance is similar to piecing together a puzzle rather than punching through a solution. This is why *How to Kill Your Batman* and *How to Conquer Your Superman* are so useful for male survivors. Due to the traumas of being sexually abused and the similarities of the two coping mechanisms, a male survivor's ability to come to terms with their trauma may sometimes teeter between hypervigilance and perfectionism, depending on the situation. While both strategies may have benefited the survivor in the past, they cannot be sustained forever. Just as Batman and Superman's methods of justice became too old-fashioned for the rest of the world, so will the survivor's ability to remain hypervigilant or seek perfectionism. When this occurs, the only option is to seek healing to eliminate the need for your Superman facade and the hypervigilance of your Dark Knight, ensuring it never rises again.

The Superman Facade and the Potential for Good

Superman, beyond the shadow of a doubt, is a hero. In fact, to many, he is *the* hero. No one else can compare. His superhero code of needing and wanting to do the right thing, no matter what the cost, is what inspires others to become the best versions of themselves. For this reason, you, as an adult survivor of childhood sexual abuse, may be reluctant to dismiss your need to maintain the Superman facade.

The Superman facade has the most potential to not only bring out the best in ourselves, but to also help guide others to become better people. There is no better example of the Superman facade's potential for good than *Action Comics* #900 (2011), "The Incident."

In this comic, Superman is under suspicion of going rogue by the United States government when he lands in the middle of an Iranian protest without authorization. On one side are Iranian pedestrians carrying picket signs and calling for reform. On the other side is the army of the Guardians of the Islamic Revolution, sporting guns and combat gear. In the middle, between both opposing forces, is where Superman lands. Amid screams of anger and military weapons, Superman does not call for a ceasefire. He does not stand with the people, ordering the military to give the people what they want. He does not stand with the military, ordering the people to disperse before blood is shed. Nor does he order everyone to stand down in order to begin dialogue and negotiations. Instead, he does nothing but stand between the two opposing forces in silence for twenty-four hours.

To explain why he chose to nearly cause an international incident that could have been construed as an act of war by the Iranian government, Superman tells the CIA operative, Gabriel

Wright, interrogating him on the grounds of Camp David in Frederick, Maryland:

As a super-hero, as Metropolis' protector, I've fought just about every threat imaginable. I'm good when it comes to fighting apocalyptic threats. But the everyday degradations that humans suffer? Dying of thirst? Hunger? People denied their basic human rights? I've never been very effective at stopping things like that. And I want to be.

After deciding to renounce his US citizenship before the United Nations, Superman tells Agent Wright:

I'm an alien, Mr. Wright. Born on another world. I can't help but see the bigger picture. I've been thinking too small. I realize that now. You asked me if my showboating was worth it. If it effected any meaningful change. Maybe not on the macro scale. But as I was flying away, I looked down and saw something. Two men. A member of the Army of the Guardian of the Islamic Revolution and a protestor. The protestor was extending a rose to the soldier. I thought the soldier was going to fire, but he did something unexpected and incredibly brave.

The representation of Superman in this comic is why so many fans across the world adore the Man of Steel. It is not because he can fly or look through walls. It is because of his belief in honesty and goodness that rarely wavers. The comic symbolizes why Superman is the iconic image of hope, a symbol of the desire to strive and become better, and a need to hold ourselves to a higher standard in an attempt to uplift others. It is for these reasons as a boy I fell in love with Superman. It is why as a man I'm still in love with Superman. He makes me want to be better.

Unfortunately, there is a problem with looking up to Superman as a role model. He is a fictional character who does not exist. While being raised in Smallville, Kansas, Jonathan and Martha Kent may have guided Clark to become a hero, but the schemas, codes, and beliefs of male survivors have a higher likelihood of seeing the world through a fractured lens of pain, guilt, shame, anger, and false truths. These male survivors seek perfectionism as a mask to hide their Superman facade.

Perfectionism in *Superman: For All Seasons*

Jeph Loeb and Tim Sale are a lot like the dynamic duo of comic book creation. Together, they do an excellent job of describing the evolution of Superman from Smallville to Metropolis in *Superman: For All Seasons*. They explain with remarkable old-fashioned style and timeless narrative how Superman came to exist and how his character grew stronger as a savior and as a means for Clark to find meaning to his life. While highlighting the positives of the superhero, Loeb and Sale also demonstrate the consequences of the Superman facade when the possibility of perfectionism is not an option.

Throughout much of the modern Superman mythos, and in *Superman: For All Seasons*, prior to the arrival of Superman, Metropolis was Lex Luthor's city. In the eyes of its denizens, he was the city's savior and protector. He provided the city with jobs and technology. In exchange, all they had to provide was their undying love, trust, and loyalty. All of this changed when Superman arrived. With the Big Blue Boy Scout present to save the people of Metropolis from Russian missiles and chemical fires, Lex Luthor no longer saw himself as the city's savior. It was not until after Superman had Lex put in jail for a single night that the shame of being second best pushed the villain over the edge to seek revenge in the most unlikely of ways. Rather than cause Superman bodily harm, which he knew he could not do effectively, he sought to fight a battle of the minds in which he knew he was more equipped to handle.

First, Lex brainwashed the biochemist, Ms. Jenny Vaughn, by locking her in a room with her eyes taped open, watching continuous videos of Superman saving innocent people from harm. The reason being, following her rescue by the Man of Steel from a chemical fire, she saw Superman as her angel. Using her admiration for Superman as leverage, Lex convinces her that her knowledge of viral infections is going to bring happiness and require Superman to need her help one day to save more innocent people.

Next, Lex releases a virus into the air of Metropolis that shuts down a person's upper respiratory system, forcing Superman to ask Lex Luthor for help. This strips Superman of his power of control and is evident when Lex narrates to the reader, "The prospect of failure is too overwhelming for him. He cannot lose faith in himself or he is lost. And lost is exactly where I want him to be."

Finally, Lex convinces Superman to fly Ms. Vaughn (now known as Toxin) over the city to apply a unique mixture of chemicals into the clouds as an antidote to the virus. The two are successful, but at the cost of Vaughn's life. On the roof of Lex Corp, standing over Superman who is kneeling beside the body of Toxin, Lex tells Superman:

> They say you can change the course of mighty rivers. But you have so little understanding of how fragile the human condition is. How easily a life, all life, can be lost. Being the most powerful man in the world means nothing if you are all alone. No one knows that better than I. Go back to wherever you came from before you fail us all.

Afterward, Superman flies away. He returns to Smallville feeling weak and filled with shame at having failed to save a person's life.

It is true, Superman is the strongest being on Earth, but there are still things outside of the hero's control. He can run faster than a speeding bullet, but he cannot cure world hunger. Sure, he can leap a building in a single bound, but he cannot cure cancer. The Man of Steel can fly, melt objects with his heat vision, and freeze objects with his ice breath, but he cannot stop the evils of human nature from manifesting themselves across the globe. This is not only true of Superman, but of male survivors of childhood sexual abuse as well.

As a survivor, you may have been sexually abused or assaulted as a child. When this occurred, you were stripped of your power and sense of being in control of your own life. This left you feeling weak and directionless. To regain the power that was stripped away, you may have attempted to mask your fear and shame using the illusion of perfectionism to appear calm and in control. Although you, as a male survivor, may attempt to hide behind the facade of perfectionism, this is not healing the trauma of the past. Instead, it is only attempting to push it down to hide the shame of being a male survivor.

There is only one way to move beyond the need to perpetuate the Superman facade. Until the Superman facade is allowed to associate with the self, you will continue to seek perfectionism not only in your life, but in the lives of those around you. This is done in an attempt to remain in control and in power to hide feelings of fear, shame, guilt, and isolation. There is no better example of how any hero can become a villain if the Superman facade is left unchecked than *Superman: Red Son* (2003).

Superman: Red Son and Becoming the Villain

Mention Superman, and for many, truth, justice, and the American way comes to mind. His belief in honesty and equity are the foundations of American society, right? What if Superman was not raised in Smallville, Kansas, by Jonathan and Martha Kent? Would he still uphold justice? Would he still embody truth? Or, would he represent something and someone entirely different? What if he were Russian? These are the questions Mark Millar raises in the graphic novel *Superman: Red Son*.

In *Red Son's* alternate reality, not only is Superman Russian, but Lois Lane is married to Lex Luthor, and although Batman is still Batman, he also hails from "The Motherland." On the surface, Millar's story is an excellent example of identifying what makes Superman great, but it also offers an example of how the need for perfection rather than growth can transform even the greatest heroes into their worst enemy.

In part one of *Superman: Red Son*, "Red Son: Rising," Superman is still Superman. Although he is Russian, the moral and heroic code of the Man of Steel remains intact. However, there are some differences. Lex Luthor is the lead scientist for the American government under the Eisenhower Administration, Lois Lane is his wife, and Wonder Woman has replaced Lois as Superman's potential love interest. Another key difference is that the facades of Clark Kent and Kal-El are nonexistent. Superman has no need to hide behind the clumsy persona of a bumbling reporter or honor the culture of a dead civilization. All Millar reveals about Comrade Superman's origin is when Superman tells another Soviet (who killed Batman's parents):

> Actually, the powers didn't start until a few weeks after my twelfth birthday, Captain Roslov. My super-hearing was the first to develop. I heard what I thought were voices in my head until I realized I was just listening to children in the next collective. Up until that point, I was just an ordinary little boy with bruised knees and a wheezy cough and a crush on my cute redheaded neighbor, just like anyone else. If I'd had the powers, I'd have left the farms years before now. But I didn't. You know why? Because my parents wanted me to be ready when I went to the big city.

Superman does good to try and protect everyone across the world, not just Russia. He wants to help. Nothing more. In fact, Comrade Superman has the same optimism as Clark Kent in *Superman: For All Seasons* and *Superman: American Alien*. He does not want to rule or control the lives of others. However, the rest of Russia wishes for him to be their ruler when Joseph Stalin passes away. Rather than accept the position of leadership, Superman remains humble, telling Captain Pyotr Roslov, "I came to Moscow to care for the people. I'm a worker, not a public speaker." He later narrates to the reader, "My heart told me to lead them, but my head told me that this completely contradicted everything my parents had ever raised me to believe in."

Similar to a male survivor's Superman facade, Superman's beliefs in *Superman: Red Son* take time coming into being, maturing, and eventually transforming for the worse. This transformation begins for Superman when he speaks with his childhood crush, Lana Lazarenko, as she stands in a breadline to receive food for her family. Using his influence, he attempts to get food only for Lana and her children, but soon the pleas from the crowd are too loud for him to ignore. Superman is confused when it is reported that, due to Stalin's death, grain will not arrive for the remainder of the month. Lana says, "It's okay, Superman. It's not your fault. It's just the way the system works, you know. You can't take care of everyone's problems." And Lana is correct. No matter how strong or "super" an individual may be, they cannot fix all the problems of others.

Unfortunately, Superman, like many male survivors who are perfectionists, does not see or understand this. Instead, perfectionists see a problem that must be fixed, that they can fix, either because of their abilities or the angle from which they view a problem. For this reason, Superman responds in the same way many male survivors would respond:

Actually, I can, Lana. I could take care of everyone's problems if I ran this place and, to tell you the truth, there's no good reason why I shouldn't. Tell your friends they don't have to be scared or hungry anymore, comrades. Superman is here to rescue them.

However, if this code of "right" is enforced with "might" rather than understanding and guidance, it can transform any hero, even Superman, into the villain of their own story.

Words matter. The words we say to ourselves and the words we say to others. They not only dictate our reactions, but the intentions behind those actions. It is for this reason, in this moment, as Superman flies into the darkened sky of Russia with hammer and sickle emblazoned on his chest as citizens cheer from below, that he is no longer there to help those in need. He is there to "rescue" them from the lives they live rather than guide them to have, develop, and live a better life. The perfectionism of the Superman facade as a male survivor believes this is what others want and what is best. This is because, as a child, you wished to be rescued from the trauma of your past. You wished for a Superman who would fly from the sky and save you, so as an adult you may attempt to be that savior that never came for you. While these intentions can be noble, as an adult these thoughts have the potential to become the negative actions of a traumatized boy seeking to force his beliefs on others. Perfectionists attempt to bring order to the chaos of their world that occurred after being sexually abused or assaulted. With order comes control. With control comes security. With security comes safety that was taken away. If the need for perfectionism continues without proper healing of the childhood trauma, male survivors begin to behave in the same way as Comrade Superman throughout the remainder of *Superman: Red Son*.

In "Red Son: Ascendant," Superman seeks to achieve a more "just" and "perfect" world after defeating the alien Brainiac who teams up with Lex Luthor to shrink and bottle the people of Stalingrad. Eventually, Superman's need for perfectionism of himself and his country was not enough. Soon, there was a need to also control the surrounding countries, which he does. The only countries that refuse to succumb to Superman's dictatorship are America and Chile. Although poverty and disease have (for the most part) been eliminated, no one strives to become better. Everyone has become complacent, knowing Superman will be there to set everything right. He explains this to Wonder Woman when he says:

Sometimes I wonder if Luthor and the Americans are right, Diana. Perhaps we do interfere with humanity too much. Nobody wears a seatbelt anymore. Ships have even stopped carrying life jackets. I don't like this unhealthy new way that people are behaving. The K.G.B. are always pushing me to take more and more control, but I already feel like I'm holding on too tight. Sometimes I worry the people don't even like me.

Superman's words demonstrate multiple problems with seeking perfectionism as a result of the Superman facade. First, individuals who seek to achieve perfection for themselves begin to resent others who do not attempt to live up to the same standards. Superman demonstrates this in the comic when he lobotomizes those who do not comply with his definition of perfection, becoming continuously happy and complacent robots who serve Superman. His words and actions also demonstrate that if the control of perfectionism continues unchecked, it also impairs the growth of others. This was shown when Superman's continued control results in the death of Batman and of Wonder Woman being stripped of her powers, age, beauty, and intelligence.

Finally, in "Red Son: Setting," the world becomes a utopia by the standards of Superman. The only country that is not under Superman's rule is America. Superman dictates the perfection of his society, and even that is not enough when he says:

On my sixty-third birthday, Brainiac calculated that the world now contained almost six billion Communists. I quickly double-checked and he was right. Moscow ticktocked with the same Swiss watch precision in every other town and city in our global Soviet Union. Every adult had a job, every child had a hobby, and the entire human population enjoyed the full eight hours sleep which their bodies required. Crime didn't exist. Accidents never happened. It didn't even rain unless Brainiac was absolutely certain that everyone was carrying an umbrella. Almost six million citizens and hardly anyone complained. Even in private. All I had to do was bide my time, and the whole world would finally be as perfect as God had intended it to be.

The world is perfect, but not perfect *enough*. With Lex Luthor as president of the United States, the US economy and its people thrive.

In Russia, Superman still has not found a way to enlarge the city and people of Stalingrad. Both of these facts make Superman's idea of perfectionism an impossibility. All the while, he believes he is doing what is best for humanity and is why he refuses to invade North America. He wants them to join his nation willingly. He even chastises Brainiac for shrinking Stalingrad and its people before being reprogrammed when he says, "How could you do this, Brainiac? What kind of monster would trap an entire civilization inside a sample jar? It's the most grotesque thing I've ever seen. You took away what made them human, and there's never an excuse for that, Brainiac."

It is Lex who helps Superman to understand that his entire career has been a black spot on the growth of humanity. Moments before the fall of the United States, Lex writes Superman a letter that reads, "Why don't you just put the whole world in a bottle, Superman?" On his knees with tears in his eyes, Superman realizes that his need to stop war and famine made him just as evil as the villain Brainiac. Like the supercomputer, Superman cared for humanity and only wished to provide them with the tools needed to survive and live a perfect life. However, in Lex's words, Superman saw that surviving was not living, and perfection was not as important as growth. Similar to Superman, survivors who live a life behind a Superman facade seek to control the actions of others, and they begin with the best of intentions. However, over time the faults and problems are all they can see. This was Superman's problem and the mistake of many male survivors who strive to live a life of perfectionism. They ignore the growth and individuality of themselves and others out of necessity to feel safe and always in control. Lex Luthor saves the world in *Superman: Red Son* with his belief that Superman limits the potential of humanity's growth. This has always been true, and the comic *Luthor* (2015) explains why individuals who may be seen as villains are sometimes not the true enemies.

Luthor and Stifling Growth for Perfectionism

Every villain is the hero of their own story. Brian Azzaerllo proves this to be true in _Luthor_. Similar to _Superman: Red Son_, _Luthor_ offers a different perspective to the consequence of perfectionism sought by survivors attempting to live behind a Superman facade.

In this comic, readers view Superman through the eyes of his enemy, the villain Lex Luthor. Superman is not drawn with a smile and well-quaffed hair. Instead, the hero is drawn to look more like a demon than a savior. He does not smile, he scowls. His eyes glow with red beams as each muscle appears inflated, exaggerated, shaded, and grotesque. The Man of Steel does not embody hope. He represents the destruction of the human race. Superman does not speak, and it is for this reason he appears to be the harbinger of doom as Lex narrates his actions. He says:

> You've been referred to by some as the world's greatest Boy Scout fighting for truth, justice, and the American Way. As if that were some inseparable holy trinity. Truth? That's in the teller. Just calmly messaged words that very well may be nothing but carefully finessed lies. Justice? Belongs to the judge, who sits above those who put him there because they can't trust themselves. And the American way? It constantly evolves out of something that proves to be true and a lie, just and more...all men are created equal. All men. You are not a man, but they've made you their hero and they worship you. So tell me what redemption do you offer them? Those red eyes, I'm sure they look straight through me, like I am nothing more than a nuisance. But when I see you, I see something no man can ever be. I see the end. The end of our potential. The end of our achievements. The end of our dreams. You are my nightmare.

I hate to say it, but everything Lex Luthor says in this passage is true.

When obstacles are eliminated, there is no growth. Superman has the potential to make others lazy in the same way the people become complacent in *Superman: Red Son,* allowing the Superman facade to live and achieve perfectionism means remaining afraid, becoming the villain, and limiting the growth of others due to the development of cognitive distortions.

After being sexually abused, the world makes little to no sense. You, the survivor, believe the abuse was your fault. For this reason, some survivors seek to perfect their Superman facade. The shame of being sexually abused forces them to create the facade of an individual that makes them feel safe and the world comprehensible. Forcing themselves to seek perfection means that they try to eliminate the shame they feel by being the best in everything they do. Unfortunately, this means hindering the growth of others. As a father and a husband, it means attempting to force others to live up to your definition of perfectionism. Those closest who care for you begin to resent you, and you resent them. Seeking perfectionism over growth ensures isolation, loneliness, and separation that can only be overcome by conquering the Superman facade.

Chapter Seven: Conquering the Superman Facade

"Yes, you're angry, but in that anger, you're forgetting once more what humans feel. What they fear. They won't forgive you for this, Clark. Forgive yourself."

Norman McCay—*Kingdom Come* (2008)

When thinking of ridding yourself of the Superman facade, you may picture a reality similar to the one imagined in *Action Comics #368* (1968) "The Unemployed Superman." Unlike *Superman #247* (1972) "Must There Be a Superman?", where the Guardians tell Superman he is hindering the growth of humanity, "The Unemployed Superman" flips the situation on its head. Rather than being asked to fix all the problems of the people, the earth exists in a state of utopia no longer in need of Superman.

In the comic, Superman finds that world peace has been achieved while he is off world. Police officers no longer patrol, fires are nonexistent, and other natural disasters have all come to an end. When Superman assumes the identity of Clark Kent, the only newsworthy event is a chess tournament. Even enemies such as Jax-Ur and Mr. Mxyzptlk have turned over a new leaf. To ensure lasting peace after Superman discovers an alien race known as the Sentinels is the cause of the new utopian society, he exiles himself to a planet with a red sun, never to return.

This issue of *Superman* makes readers question what happens when a person's wildest dreams are achieved. Similar to parents who find themselves directionless when their children have ventured out to start lives of their own, Superman finds himself questioning his purpose if he is not saving the world from danger. For this reason, some male survivors may be reluctant to put their

Superman facade to rest. Similar to Superman, male survivors may believe they will no longer be needed or useful if they do not function behind a mask of perfectionism. They may believe they need their Superman to live and be happy, but this is not true. The only way to achieve peace from a traumatic past of childhood sexual abuse is to become a complete individual, free of facades. This truth can best be seen in the graphic novel *Huck* (2001) by Mark Millar. *Huck* is not a Superman comic, per se. Instead, it's a book that helps to describe (in my opinion) what Superman could be.

In the book, the main character, Huck, has many of the same abilities as Superman. He has super strength and can run at incredible speeds, but he cannot fly. He also has one ability Superman does not. With a name, picture, or vivid description, Huck can find any missing object or person. Also, unlike Superman, Huck does not attempt to be a superhero. He does not wear a costume, hide his identity, or conceal his powers. Instead, he attempts to accomplish one good deed a day from his job as a gas station attendant.

When Huck's special abilities are made public, the character remains the same. He does not change. Instead of denying his abilities, he sees it as an opportunity to help more people than those in his small town.

The publicity of his abilities should have changed the way he sees himself and the way he interacts with others. Instead, he remains true to who he is. He does not become a promotional gimmick for the mayor's reelection campaign. Nor does he trade in his jean jacket for a fancy suit and tie or quit his job at the gas station to live off the perks of his powers. Knowing he is being used, Huck leaves the mayor high and dry during his fundraiser, but not before feeding the stray cats outside his window with his room service and offering his hotel room to homeless men to ensure they get a good night's sleep.

Unlike Superman, Huck does not develop an alternate facade to blend in with the crowd or protect those closest to him from harm by guarding the secret of his powers. His personality remains intact as he refuses to live behind the mask of a false identity. As a male survivor seeking to heal from the trauma of childhood sexual abuse, the goal of learning to conquer your Superman is associating (merging) your dissociated identity. It is the only way to progress from a fractured victim to a complete survivor.

This final part of the Superman facade addresses the ability to heal from past traumas and the strategies that can be accomplished to mend a fractured facade. To explain the path toward healing your Superman facade and defeating the need for perfectionism, *Injustice: Gods Among Us: Year One* (2013) will be used to explain cognitive distortions and how to change negative automatic thoughts into positive truths.

Injustice

What happens when someone loses all that they care for, and all they have ever loved is stripped away? Does it strip away all that they were, leaving a hollow shell disguised as a monster in its wake? It does for Superman in *Injustice: Gods Among Us: Year One* (2013).

Injustice is an epic saga that spans multiple years, documenting Superman's decent from hero to villain as he strives to rid the world of crime. His fall from grace begins with the villain, Joker. In "Year One," the Joker uses a mixture of a scarecrow's fear toxin and kryptonite to convince Superman he was being attacked by the villain Doomsday. To put the villain out of commission quickly, he flies the villain into space. Before he realizes what has happened, it is too late. Lois dies while also killing her and Superman's unborn child. Unfortunately, the tragedy does not stop there. Killing Lois also triggers the detonation of a nuclear warhead in Metropolis, killing everyone in the city and making it a nuclear wasteland the moment Lois's heart ceases to beat.

In a single day, Superman has lost his wife, his child, the city he swore to protect, and all of the friends he knew as Clark Kent. All that trauma in a single instant pushes the superhero over the edge. No longer is he a hero of optimism and hope. Instead, he becomes a person who seeks perfection in his ability to provide protection, safety, and order to the rest of the world at any cost, including murder. To achieve what he believes to be justice, Superman punches a hole through Joker's chest, killing him instantly. This action begins Superman's descent into becoming a villain and is sealed when he kills the hero, Green Arrow.

This comic, more than any other, demonstrates what happens when the Superman facade is no longer an option for a male survivor as a coping strategy. When the safety of control offered by the possibility of perfectionism cannot be achieved, the hero quickly becomes a villain in the same way a survivor quickly becomes a victim. Not because the hero or the survivor wishes to become their own worst enemy, but because they never healed from the trauma of their past.

Using Superman's act of murder as a guide, this chapter explores how to understand and heal cognitive distortions and conquer the need for the Superman facade. However, before being capable of transforming negative thoughts into positive affirmations, we need to understand the difference between a survivor and a victim.

Victim vs. Survivor

Understanding the abuse you may have suffered means not only understanding the nature of the abuse, but also what and how you define who you were, what you are, and who you wish to become. The title of this guide is *How to Conquer Your Inner Superman*. The nature of this book's content and its use of superheroes and villains to heal childhood trauma implies that the reality in which we live consists of good guys and bad guys, heroes and villains. Unfortunately, this is not true. The stories we read, tell, watch, and create have a protagonist on one side and an antagonist on the other. However, our lives are filled with ordinary human beings capable of greatness and god-awful atrocities. The people we are and the individuals who surround us are capable of being both saint and sinner at any given moment. All of us, no matter who we are or where we come from, have something which frightens us, someone or something we love(d), and someone or something we have lost. The objective of this book is not to point fingers, blame, and identify someone as either a villain or a hero. Both are flawed. The objective is to help individuals understand the nature of the abuse they suffered as a child, how to heal from its repercussions, and to become a complete individual who lives in the present.

Although heroes and villains cannot be noticed in our society with capes and maniacal laughter, there are perpetrators, victims, and survivors. In fact, most perpetrators of sexual abuse were victims of sexual abuse and trauma themselves as either children or adults. This does not mean all victims of sexual abuse go on to become perpetrators. According to the Rape, Abuse, and Incest National Network (RAINN), it is just the opposite. Most male victims of childhood sexual abuse go on to be nonoffenders. Although perpetrators can easily be viewed as villains, there are also victims and survivors in the equation. While every survivor was a victim of sexual abuse, every victim is not a survivor. There is a difference between the two.

To no longer be a victim and become a survivor of childhood sexual abuse, whether male or female, means more than not being killed during or immediately following a sexual assault. To be a survivor means to heal or to work toward recovery of past sexual abuse to become a complete individual. This does not mean suppressing, denying, or dissociating from memories and knowledge of the horrific events of the past, but attempting to put in the time and work to face the horrific demons of the past. Victims blame others (including themselves) for the problems and unfortunate events that have happened in their life, while survivors hold others accountable (including themselves) for their actions along with positive and negative repercussions. Becoming a survivor is difficult, while remaining a victim can be easy but detrimental. Throughout the rest of this chapter, Superman's actions in *Injustice* will be used to understand the difference between hero, villain, victim, and how to begin the process of conquering the need to hide behind the mask of a Superman facade.

Cognitive Behavioral Therapy (CBT)

Trauma that occurs in the past does not stay in the past. While it may seem the trauma of childhood sexual abuse can be hidden behind a Superman facade as a coping mechanism because it has worked in the past, this is not true. Repressed childhood trauma has an impact on the present, not only in mental health, but in physical health as well. Dr. Bessel Van der Kolk explains in his bestselling book, *The Body Keeps the Score*, that a survivor may deny that the body tends to harbor these memories and express them in the form of physical pain. In some cases, a survivor may not even remember a trauma occurred until the body experiences a similar sensation that triggers a memory of past trauma. This is called state-dependent recall. If past trauma continues to be denied into adulthood, it can manifest itself in the form of chronic pain. This is because although chronic pain is physical, it also has a psychological aspect that cannot be healed without changing the way a survivor thinks about themselves, others, society, and their interactions with all the above. One way to heal is through the use of **Cognitive Behavioral Therapy (CBT)**.

To overcome the need to live life behind the mask of a Superman facade, a survivor must develop the ability to transform negative thoughts into true statements free of cognitive distortions. This cannot be accomplished overnight. It takes time, practice, patience, and the help of a trained psychiatrist, therapist, or counselor in Cognitive Behavioral Therapy.

Cognitive behavioral therapy has become increasingly popular for trauma survivors of C-PTSD because it addresses the link between thoughts, feelings, and actions. CBT helps to address the problematic thinking and beliefs many survivors have about themselves, their actions, and others (cognitive), which result in negative feelings and actions of themselves and others (behavioral).

Another reason CBT is popular among trauma survivors is because it teaches survivors to be their own therapist. The step-by-step way it is taught ensures the survivor is active in their own healing. This helps to decrease feelings of helplessness and low self-worth associated with being a survivor, reducing the risk of paralyzing depression. However, while CBT does teach survivors to eventually be their own therapist, the ability to use the strategies of CBT effectively must be taught by a trained therapist. The exercises below can be accomplished independently, but also use them to discuss your thoughts, actions, and feelings with your therapist, counselor, or psychiatrist.

Superman and Cognitive Distortions

The first step in using CBT is to understand and identify cognitive distortions. These are "thinking errors" that are a result of false beliefs developed over time due to past trauma. For male survivors, these negative automatic thoughts lead to the belief that the sexual abuse of the past was their fault, and that if they truly wanted to prevent the sexual abuse they could have. Coping with these negative thoughts as a boy meant denying the past abuse ever took place and developing the Superman facade. As an adult, denial is no longer effective as a coping mechanism, and the only lasting solution is addressing these cognitive distortions. For many male survivors to conquer their need to hide behind a Superman facade they must learn to recognize these cognitive distortions:

All-or-Nothing Thinking: Things are viewed in absolute black-and-white categories. This means there can only be a right and a wrong answer, with no gray areas in between. These thoughts lead some survivors to view themselves as being either a hero or villain. All-or-nothing thinking falls most closely in line with the need for perfectionism. Male survivors living a life behind a Superman facade believe actions and beliefs must be one way or the other with no gray area in between. To grow and heal, survivors must move beyond all-or-nothing thinking and examine situations completely to understand the full effects of their thoughts on their actions.

Evidence of all-or-nothing thinking and perfectionism can be demonstrated by Superman on the last page of *Injustice* "Part One." Superman stands at a podium before the United Nations, reveals his secret identity, and tells the world that either they choose to stop crime and war, or he will put an end to it. With the shirtless dictator of Bialya on his knees at his side, Superman tells the audience:

> As a journalist, I spent too much time writing about the evil in the world. As a hero, I have spent too much time reacting to evils already perpetrated. No more. What happened yesterday can never be allowed to happen again. Monsters can no longer roam free among us. This man turned his weapons against his own people. He is a criminal and he will be tried as one. To those who would do the same, those who would hurt others, know that I will come for you. I don't care about your lands or your beliefs. I don't care about your petty squabbles. I don't care if you're a madman or a terrorist, a king or a president. You do not have the right to take innocent lives. I am calling for an immediate world-wide ceasefire. All hostiles stop immediately— or I will stop them. It's over.

The speech is powerful and terrifying. It also shows the problems in all-or-nothing thinking.

All-or-nothing thinking leads to the disregard of other people's feelings, thoughts, and beliefs. Perfectionism and all-or-nothing thinking lead to thoughts of "I don't care," as stated by Superman.

This limits the growth of others and shuts down the possibility of dialogue. This also makes others believe failure cannot be an option, when failure must be an option. It is the only way to ensure future growth rather than absolute thinking. Flash demonstrates to Superman the potential impact of all-or-nothing thinking while playing Superman in a game of chess.

Superman tells Flash he wants to get rid of all guns. Rather than say this is wrong, Flash equates gun deaths to the number of deaths caused by cigarettes. He says:

> Smoking. Cigarettes. They kill far more people than guns. People keep smoking even when they know it's killing them. They keep smoking and looking into the eyes of their families and they die . . . And tomorrow we get rid of cigarettes . . . You want to save lives? That's how we do it. Then we imprison anyone who speeds in a car . . . Then we lock up anyone who leaves a dangerous dog unchained . . . Then we kill anyone who doesn't recycle.

All-or-nothing thinking is a slippery slope that can lead to negative outcomes when looking at the world through a lens of black-and-white thinking. Superman's view of good and bad and right and wrong is according to his own hero code rather than truth. This is evident when he says, "I don't care if you're a madman or a terrorist, a king or a president. You do not have the right to take innocent lives." To heal means changing these thoughts to become more inclusive and open to the opinions and beliefs of others.

Overgeneralizations: A negative event is viewed as a never-ending pattern of defeat or a simplification of circumstances. This means that survivors view actions and themselves through the lens of a victim rather than a survivor. The automatic thoughts of a victim believe the world is always against them and there is no way to win, so why try? A victim may also simplify their thoughts to justify their actions. This sense of isolation and defeatism only leads to shame because the survivor could not prevent the sexual abuse.

In the case of Superman, his shame originates in his inability to prevent the death of Lois Lane or the people of Metropolis. This is shown in *Injustice: Year One* "Part Twelve" when Jor-El tells Superman he has killed. Rather than be accountable for his actions, he tells his father, "They hurt Diana. They tried to murder me! I had no choice, Father." Jor-El's response is, "There is always a choice," and he is right. There is always a choice. Whether it is right or wrong is another question. The key to healing this cognitive distortion is holding yourself and others accountable for their actions, whether they be positive or negative.

Magnification or Minimization: The survivor blows situations out of proportion or shrinks their importance. This means placing value in the wrong place. While the emotions of a survivor may be minimized, the importance of others may be inflated in some instances, allowing them to remain unnoticed and protected through invisibility. In other circumstances, it means continuing to identify as a victim through perfectionism to maintain a sense of control.

Superman is the victim of both forms of cognitive distortions in *Injustice: Gods Among Us*. He minimizes his own negative actions while magnifying the actions of others. A good example of how magnification and minimization can impact a survivor's view of themselves and others can be seen in a conversation between Superman and Batman. Superman tells Batman:

You can't possibly understand what he took. He stole the life Lois and I would have had together. Our child. And more. There was going to be someone else like me in the world. Another Kryptonian. Someone who would have made me feel less alone. And I would have loved that child more than anything. I already did. And look at you. You're sitting in the dark ignoring Dick and Damian. How many friends did they have in Metropolis? Have you consoled them? Have you held them? Your parents died and left you, Bruce. What's your excuse for not being a father?

Victims believe the trauma of their past is a pain no one else can understand. This strengthens the Superman facade's belief that others need them to be perfect because no one knows "what it is like" or "what they have lost." Superman believes his pain is greater than Batman's. He believes Batman could not know the pain of losing a son because he has two. However, he does not know the pain, shame, and guilt Batman has had to cope with since childhood.

Superman's words help to show that this cognitive distortion magnifies beliefs of what is right and wrong to protect others, while minimizing other's feelings who may have also suffered trauma. While being a male survivor of childhood sexual abuse may offer you a unique perspective because of the pain you suffered as a child, it does not mean you can ignore and minimize the feelings of others. It lessens others, preventing growth and healing of yourself and others. To heal means recognizing a common humanity between you and others. It means knowing that each individual suffers, grieves, mourns, and heals in their own way. However, it does not mean hurting, judging, or minimizing others (or yourself) in the process.

Personalization and Blame: The survivor blames himself for something he wasn't entirely responsible for, or he blames others while denying his role in the problem. In either circumstance, it means playing the victim. It ensures a semblance of control through a false belief of control and accountability that was never his own, or righteousness in the false belief that he is completely innocent of all wrongdoing because of the sexual abuse endured in his past resulting in the victimization of his present. This cognitive distortion is seen in *Injustice: Gods Among Us: Year One* when Batman organizes a group of heroes to break into Superman's Fortress of Solitude to steal a pill that is being manufactured to give humans temporary super abilities. Superman hopes to use these pills to create a superpowered military to help police the world.

In the final pages of the graphic novel, Green Arrow manages to attach one of the pills to an arrow and shoot it to Batman and the other heroes waiting in the distance. Unfortunately, in order to distract Superman from his true intentions, he deflected an arrow off of Superman's chest and into the shoulder of Jonathan Kent, Superman's adoptive father. Filled with rage after the death of Lois Lane, his unborn child, and the nuclear destruction of Metropolis, Superman pummels Green Arrow's skull into a bloody pulp. This action, quite literally, places Green Arrow's blood on Superman's hands.

Afterward, rather than accepting responsibility for murdering Green Arrow, Superman tells his adoptive mother, Martha Kent:

> I didn't mean to . . . I . . . he hurt you . . . This was his fault. Batman led them here. He has been working against me this whole time. He let Lois die . . . He let Joker live. He let him escape again and again. All the wars we've stopped, all the deaths we've prevented. Bruce would see it all go back to the way it was. As long as he lives he will stand against me.

Surrounding Superman, each of his parents attempts to talk reason into their son. The hologram of Jor-El says that Batman "Would have humanity determine its own path. I'm sorry, Kal. He is right in this." Martha Kent says, "Bruce is your friend. Please don't take his life." Rather than listen to any of them, Superman flies away to take down Batman. Each is left standing consoling the other, wondering where they went wrong. Martha says to Jor-El, "We tried to raise your son. We're so sorry." Jor-El responds, "I'm sorry I unleashed this on your world."

As a male survivor, you may have found yourself in the same situation as Superman. While in a state of rage you may have done or said something you are not proud of. Afterward, you realize what you have done is wrong, but rather than apologize, you deny your involvement and double down on your schemas. You blame others for your actions in the same way Superman blames Batman for the loss of Lois and for Green Arrow's death.

On the other hand, you may not blame others in the same way Superman blames himself. Instead, you may turn the rage inward and blame yourself in the same way Superman's parents blame themselves for their son's actions, rather than holding him accountable for his actions. Rather than expressing rage outward on others in the same way Superman punched Green Arrow into a bloody pulp on the floor of the Fortress of Solitude, you hold the rage in, creating feelings of guilt and shame for who you are. Both lead to strengthening the Superman facade and further disassociation rather than association of the self. The only way to heal is to recognize and understand these cognitive distortions and to transform the negative thoughts into positive affirmations.

Parent, Child, and Adult Thoughts

In *Injustice: Gods Among Us*, Martha Kent tells Lex Luthor a story of when Superman was a boy and could not control his anger. She explains:

Clark had a blanket when he was a child. He carried it everywhere. He slept with it. He couldn't be separated from it. The thing was filthy but he'd scream anytime I tried to wash it. Then, one day, he lost his blanket. We never saw it again. Clark was so upset. And that was the day—the day we first discovered what Clark can do.

The images show Clark as a toddler flipping over a tractor in anger. Similar to Clark as a child, male survivors who have not healed remain perpetually in the mental state of an adult child due to the impact of their childhood sexual abuse.

An *adult child* is a grown individual who continues to behave and think in the same way as a child. These individuals usually have difficulty finding their place and understanding the world due to their childhood trauma and a refusal to enter the healing process to mourn the loss of their childhood. Instead, they treat their inner child with disrespect, calling them horrible names and expressing hatred for being too weak to prevent the childhood trauma of the past. The survivor locks their inner child away, causing bursts of rage similar to the anger expressed by Superman. This is because as a child the survivor locked their inner child away in hopes of becoming what is believed to be a real man, in hopes of restoring the safety that was taken away by their abuser. Unfortunately, this also may mean locking away the need to have emotions or trust in others in the same trusting manner as children. The falsehood of the belief of being a "real man" may not become fully aware until the birth of a child, or when a child in the care of a survivor reaches the age in which the survivor was sexually abused. When this happens, the survivor may find themselves becoming a villain rather than a hero as they experience moments of rage and anxiety without warning, similar to Superman as a child. One possible cure is to make peace with the inner child and transform the cognitive distortions of negative thoughts into true statements absent of distortions. Altering the cognitive distortions and reframing automatic thoughts to those of an adult rather than a hurt child will create better mental health and long-term lasting happiness.

Male survivors may often find themselves saying to their inner child, "Stop being so weak," "You can push harder than that," and "You'll still have more you can give and do if you stop holding back!" These statements are abusive to the inner child and continue the thought of having little to no self-worth. These thoughts cannot be accomplished overnight, but the abuse of the inner child must be recognized. When harsh words are being directed at the inner child, change the words to those of praise and encouragement. Make peace in the knowledge that the very best is being done and that nothing more can be asked. When this understanding is reached, the inner child will no longer be viewed as the bad guy but as a person deserving love and support, the same as anyone else. Then you, as a male survivor of childhood sexual abuse, will truly know the sexual abuse was in no way your fault and that you did not have the strength to stop it then, but you are strong now.

A simple strategy to help change distorted automatic thoughts can be to label and change them from the thoughts of a child or parent to that of an adult.

Childish Thoughts: These thoughts are filled with excuses and passing of blame to others. For example, after murdering Green Arrow, Superman tells his parents, "Batman led them here. He has been working against me this whole time. He let Lois die . . . He let Joker live. He let him escape again and again." Rather than being accountable for his actions, he blames his rage on Batman and his perceived shortcomings as a superhero. Your thoughts may be the same way. Rather than explore your role in the possible problem and holding yourself accountable, you believe your actions are justified while looking down on the thoughts and beliefs of others who do not agree with your own.

Parental Thoughts: These thoughts are filled with "should" and "must" statements, making the survivor believe they have no choice. For example, when standing before the United Nations, Superman tells the world, "What happened yesterday can never be allowed to happen again. Monsters can no longer roam free among us." Superman is speaking as if chastising children in order to establish his control over the situation. This is to ensure the trauma he experienced never occurs again in the same way that you, as a male survivor, may attempt to achieve perfectionism to establish order and control that was taken away after being sexually abused. Similar to Superman, this is the only way you believe you are able to feel safe. Rather than acknowledge the limitations of your actions and speak positive words or encouragement to yourself, you state what must be done, giving ultimatums rather than choices.

Adult Thoughts: The goal of this exercise is to reframe automatic thoughts so that they are no longer those of an uncompromising parent or child being controlled by denial of their needs and wants. This takes practice and the help of a counselor or therapist trained in Cognitive Behavior Therapy.

Below is a writing exercise to help you recognize your cognitive distortions, analyze your childish and parental thoughts, and transform these thoughts into those of an adult. To demonstrate how to accomplish this exercise, the negative automatic thoughts of Superman in *Injustice* have been transformed to those of an adult free of cognitive distortions. If possible, work with a therapist, counselor, or support system to conquer the need for your Superman facade.

Automatic Thought Exercise				
Automatic Thought	Cognitive Distortion	Childish Reasoning	Parental Reasoning	Adult Automatic Thought
As a hero, I have spent too much time reacting to evils already perpetrated. No more. What happened yesterday can never be allowed to happen again. Monsters can no longer roam free among us.	All-or-nothing Thinking		X	What happened yesterday was a tragedy that has changed and affected us all.
They hurt Diana. They tried to murder me! I had no	Overgeneralization	X		They hurt Diana. They tried to murder me. In my

choice, Father.				anger I took another person's life.
I don't care about your lands or your beliefs. I don't care about your petty squabbles. I don't care if you're a madman or a terrorist, a king or a president. You do not have the right to take innocent lives.	All-or-nothing Thinking		X	We all have different beliefs, but we can all work together to save innocent lives.
You can't possibly understand what he took. He stole the life Lois and I would have had together.	Magnification and Minimization	X		Lois and the life we would have had was taken from me.
This was his fault.	Personalization and	X		Batman led them here,

Batman led them here. He has been working against me this whole time. He let Lois die.	Blame			but I took a person's life.

Transforming negative automatic thoughts into automatic thoughts that are free of cognitive distortions takes practice. It will not happen automatically until you are aware of your cognitive distortions and learn how to transform them into those of an adult. Norman McCoy explains this best when he tells Superman moments before attempting to kill everyone in the United Nations by collapsing the roof in *Kingdom Come* (2008):

Listen to me, Clark. Of all the things you can do, all the powers, the greatest has always been your instinctive knowledge of right and wrong. It was a gift of your own humanity. You never had to question your choices. In any situation, any crisis, you knew what to do. But the minute you made the super more important than the man, the day you decided to turn your back on mankind, that completely cost you your instinct. That took your judgment away. Take it back. If you want redemption, Clark, it lies in the very next decision you make. Make it as a man and make it right.

Placing the "super" before the "man" prevents you from achieving your full potential. Ridding yourself of cognitive distortions allows you to no longer see the world in black, white, or gray as a hero or as a villain. It allows you to view yourself and your actions through the eyes of a survivor and a good man capable of lifting others to reach their full potential as you strive to reach your own.

Chapter Eight: Conquering My Superman Facade (Autobiographical)

"I used to like having a secret. I loved it. But now . . . I've never felt so alone. No one to talk to, to share my fear with . . ."

Clark Kent—*Superman: Secret Identity* (2015)

As a male survivor, you may have felt the need to hold the world on your shoulders to be a superman. This may have meant overextending yourself and falling short of reaching your goal when you take on too many responsibilities. As a result, your lowered self-esteem may have affected your journey through the healing process. Another way to help conquer the need to live a life behind the mask of a Superman facade is through journaling to identify areas of cognitive distortions. This form of narrative writing has proven to help trauma survivors articulate their story and begin to heal.

Below are moments in my life in which I sought to achieve perfection and fell short as a father, husband, educator, and man. The first story is an excerpt from my journal, documenting my feelings of depression, anxiety, and thoughts of suicide following the death of my brother-in-law, TJ, and my attempt to be Superman. This story first appeared in *Heroes, Villains, and Healing: A Guide for Male Survivors of Childhood Sexual Abuse Using DC Superheroes and Villains* (2017). The second is one of my favorite short stories, "Action Guy," that describes what it is like to blame and imprison my inner child following my sexual abuse. It first appeared in the book of short stories *Thoughts in Italics* (2008). The third is a short story excerpt from my journal, "Cardboard," which first appeared in

Raped Black Male: A Memoir (2011). It explains depression in terms of feeling as though I were made of cardboard.

TJ

In the fall of 2016, my brother-in-law, TJ, fell sick, was remitted into hospice, and passed away two weeks afterward at the age of twenty-eight. TJ was born with the degenerative brain disease known as MPS, or Sanfilippo syndrome. It is rare and usually fatal by early adulthood.

As a boy, TJ was fully functional as a toddler. He could run, talk, eat, and play in most ways as any other toddler. However, as he grew older, his motor functions, speech, and mobility became limited. Later, he was implanted with a feeding tube and limited in movement to either his wheelchair or bed. Unfortunately, MPS strikes quickly in most children diagnosed with the disease. Most never live to see their teens and rarely reach the age of twenty. So, for TJ to live almost to his thirties is testament to his drive to live. People around him loved him, and he touched many lives.

When TJ became sick and it was evident he was not going to get better, Sarah, my wife, and my two children, Mirus and Amare, made our way to Wooster, Ohio, to be with him in his final days. Sarah spent her time in the hospice with her younger brother and parents. For over a week, TJ fought, refusing to let go, even when he was within an inch of his life and struggling to breathe. As he rallied day after day, my mother and father-in-law made the decision to take TJ home where he and the rest of the family would be more comfortable.

During the week TJ was in hospice, I was taking care of Mirus and Amare, leaving and returning to hospice when it seemed TJ was able to handle visitors. I wanted to ensure everyone was allowed to take care of themselves and mourn the losing of TJ. Days of isolation in the home of my in-laws slowly crept forward, and dealing with two toddler girls while supporting Sarah as she watched her brother wither away began to take its toll.

When TJ left hospice and returned home, I believed the entire family would make our way back to Baltimore, Maryland, then return at a moment's notice to be with TJ in his last hours. However, Sarah wanted to stay, and I agreed that it was the best decision. To ensure she did not have to worry about the girls, I decided to take them back to Baltimore with me.

At the time, I believed I could drive through the night on Sunday as Mirus and Amare slept, sleep a few hours at home, get the girls dressed and to daycare before getting to work to teach a full day with a class of seventh graders. I believed I was Superman. I could do it all. However, driving through the night and waking up the next morning to a house absent of Sarah as my brother-in-law passed away in Ohio was too much. I was able to get the girls dressed and to daycare, but I could not get to work. I spent the day sleeping, cleaning, and beating myself up for not being with my wife and not making it to work.

I was able to attend work the next day, but I cried after taking Mirus and Amare to daycare. I spoke to my mother on the phone for support, but when I arrived, I broke down. The thought of preparing to teach seventh graders, all the work that needed to be accomplished at school and at home, on top of feeling like a shitty husband and son-in-law was too much. Tears came uncontrollably as I began to have recurring thoughts of suicide. I asked my principal for a long-term substitute for my class but was told my absences were a burden to my other seventh-grade team members, so I stayed. I also wondered if I would act out my thoughts of suicide if I went home.

The next morning, TJ passed. I took my daughters to daycare, taught throughout the day, raced home to pack our bags, picked up Mirus and Amare, and drove the six hours through the night back to Wooster, Ohio.

Like Superman, I refused to admit my weaknesses and shortcomings. Instead, I tried to do it all, failed, and hated myself for it. As a survivor, I believed I needed to be perfect and accomplish everything I planned. I held a penetrating fear of losing the world I had built for myself and my family. I believed I must have a sense of control and safety, which was stripped away from me when I was raped. I had no way of accomplishing it all, so my self-esteem suffered. As a survivor of childhood sexual abuse, I must know and accept what I can and cannot do if I want to continue to heal and stay mentally healthy. Sometimes, pushing myself beyond my comfort zone helps me to succeed and become a better man. However, other times it holds me back, damaging me through negative thoughts. The key is to know when to push and when to rest.

Action Guy (Fiction)

This is my room. I got toys! I got lots of toys! Not as many as before, but I still got toys. And they're not as new as they used to be. This one's broken, but that's okay. I still like it without the siren. I don't need a siren, as long as it still rolls. I can make the siren noise. See? *Wrrr!* Got to put out the fire! Hurry! *Wrrr!* See? It still works. Even without the siren. I got other toys though. I got a sailboat, a wagon and . . . Oh! Action Guy! I love Action Guy! He can do everything. Fly, *swwiisshh*, beat up bad guys, *Bang! Pow!* Burst through walls. *Boom!* And go wherever he wants by just thinking it. I wish I had that power. Just close my eyes really tight, think really hard about some place far, far away, and, *poof*, I'm there. Anywhere! On a mountain, in the sky, in China, anywhere! That would be so cool. To go outside.

I used to go places like Action Guy. Run in the grass and play, but not anymore. Not with the door locked. The door is always locked, at least now. It wasn't before. Before the bad thing. Before . . . before the walls used to be blue, bright blue. And I had lots of toys. New toys with sounds, and lights, and cool, bright colors. There was

117

carpet, and outside my windows I could see clouds and sky and grass and sun. It was fun! But now . . . now it's different since the bad thing. I'm not supposed to talk about the bad thing. It's not like it used to be since it happened. The walls are dirty and faded. The carpet is gone, and the wood is hard and cold and creaks when I walk on it. And the clouds are gone. The windows are bricked up, and I only have one tiny little hole to look out of. And I can't see anything through it. Only sun. One small dot of sun. My toys are old, and no one comes to see me. I'm always the only person here. I like to play by myself, but sometimes . . . sometimes I wish I had someone else to make the siren noise and I didn't always have to make believe to be happy.

No one ever let me out after the bad thing. After she made me do stuff I didn't wanna do. I didn't want to play that game anyway. She made me! She said it would be fun! It wasn't fun! It was never fun. It was scary and made me feel bad. She made me touch . . . and . . . and to get on top of her. I didn't want to. I never wanted to. But I did. So, I got in trouble. I got locked in here for being bad. It's my fault. I shouldn't have done it. Now I'm being punished. No more toys, no more clouds, or sun, or fun stuff. It's all my fault. I shouldn't have done it. Now, I have to wait for someone to unlock the door. They'll come. I know they will. Action Guy will come and break down the door, kick out the bricks in the windows, and then he'll grab my hand and we'll squeeze our eyes together really right like this, and then, *poof*, we'll be outside in the sun. Flying all day and it won't be my fault no more and the bad thing will be over. But . . . but the door is still locked and Action Guy hasn't come yet, so I guess . . . I guess I'll wait and play by myself. Like I always do.

Cardboard (Fiction)

Opening eyes and seeing the steps, he was careful not to fall through the stiff, black cardboard.

He touched the white paper walls and brown paper banister. In the darkness he turned on the light. Flicking the switch like the snap of a rubber band.

The first landing was sturdier, so he walked with ease toward the white papered door and stiff cardstock handle. Gently, so not to break through like he had countless times before, he turned the handle and entered the blue and green construction-paper room. Brown paper wrapped the small couch to the left, and sitting there, smiling with the sight of his face, was his flesh and blood, living, breathing, and happy daughter that he loved with all his paper heart.

With hands and fingers of wrapping and newspaper, he reached to pick her up. Fragile fingers touched her living body and gave way to the weight. Drooping, sagging to the floor as he lifted with all the might the paste of his shoulders would allow. Each arm almost fell from his body to the floor, and for a moment he thought they would, but they held.

She nestled into his chest, denting the paper and plastic padding. There was no pain. There was nothing. Only the crackling of his flesh under her weight. The baby sought comfort and found it. He sat, battered, bruised, and dented on the four legs of the couch. She cuddled into a ball and slept in the mass of tissue paper and padding that was her father. Together they rested. Him pleased that he could at least give her a place to feel comfortable and happy, even if he had fallen apart in the process.

PART THREE:
THE KAL-EL FACADE

"You must remember you were sent here because you look like one of them—but you are not one of them."

Jor-El—*Superman: Last Son* (2008)

Although Clark Kent is the alter ego of Superman, what makes the Man of Steel unique as a comic superhero is that while most superheroes have two identities, Superman has three: Superman, Clark Kent, and Kal-El.

Superman #53, "The Origin of Superman" (1948) provides readers with Superman's origins on Krypton. The comic explains the hero's birth and his life as Kal-El with his father, Jor-El, and mother, Lara, before being placed in a rocket being sent to Earth within moments of Krypton's destruction. When the young Kryptonian landed on Earth, he was found by farmers Jonathan and Martha Kent and was given the name Clark. This means that although born on Krypton, he is a baby when he lands on Earth, too young to remember his Kryptonian origins.

Throughout childhood he is raised as a human, consistently feeling like an outsider but never understanding why. It is not until after acquiring his super abilities during adolescence that he is told he is an alien from the planet Krypton. However, even with the knowledge of being an alien, he does not know what it means to be Kryptonian. Although he researched the history of his culture and family, he never felt truly Kryptonian until *Superman #141* "Superman's Return to Krypton" (1960).

In this comic, Superman travels so fast while chasing a creature in space that he travels back in time, transporting himself to the planet Krypton prior to its destruction, his birth, and the marriage of his parents. However, because of Kyrpton's red sun, Superman is forced to land on the planet where he is unable to escape without the superpowers given to him by Earth's yellow sun.

Once on the planet, Superman meets his parents on their wedding day after being mistaken for an extra on the set of a science fiction movie due to the odd appearance of his Superman costume. He tells everyone, including his parents, that his name is Kal-El, and without much debate he is accepted as a Kryptonian. Jor-El and Lara view Kal as an equal, accepting him as a friend.

Krypton's leading actress views Kal as a lover with whom she can share her life. Kal-El does not feel like the same outsider as he did on Earth. Instead, he feels at home. In an attempt to remain on Krypton, Kal tries to save the planet from its destructive fate, but the past cannot be changed. Due to an accident on the set of a science fiction movie, Kal-El finds his way off the surface of the planet, where his powers are restored. Rather than return to Krypton and suffer the same fate of his parents and the woman he loves, Superman returns to the future.

During the time spent on Krypton without his powers and with his parents, Kal knew what it meant to not feel alone, to be accepted, and to live a life in plain sight, not behind a mask. He was accepted by his culture and people. While on Krypton, the facades of Superman and Clark Kent melted away. There was only Kal-El. However, when he returned to his own time, the new identity of Kal was solidified, making him feel more alone than ever as he attempted to not only live behind the facade of Clark Kent or attempt to live up to the impossible perfection of Superman, but attempt to live with the survivor's guilt of Kal-El.

For Superman, what it meant to be a Kryptonian was not innate. It was socialized and learned throughout his time spent on the planet with his parents. The same is true for boys. Rather than being born with an innate sense of what it means to be male, the rules of what it means to be a boy (and eventually a man) is learned over time through socialization. Similar to Superman, boys are implicitly told they will one day grow up to be men who conceal their emotions and what is needed to fulfill the cookie-cutter definition of what it means to be a "real" man. This is why many male survivors find themselves wavering between *rigid* and *unbounded boundaries* in the form of the Kal-El facade.

Chapter Nine: Understanding the Kal-El Facade

"Earth has robbed you of your potential. You are far from a Kryptonian. You are a simple brute."

Brainiac—*Superman: Brainiac* (2018)

In *Superman Annual #11* (1985), "For the Man Who Has Everything," Superman receives a birthday gift from the supervillain Mongol. The gift is called a "Black Mercy." It is described by Mongol as, "something between a plant and an intelligent fungus. It attaches itself to its victims in a form of symbiosis, feeding from their bio-aura." In essence, it reads the mind of its host to provide the person with their "heart's desire" while draining them of life. When the Black Mercy attaches to Superman, he experiences a reality in which Krypton was not destroyed. Instead of being sent to Earth in a spacecraft to be raised as Clark by Jonathan and Martha Kent, Superman is raised as Kal-El on the planet Krypton by his parents, Jor-El and Lara.

In the alternate reality created by the Black Mercy, Kal marries the movie star Lyla Lerrol. Together, Kal and Lyla have two children: a son, Van, and a daughter, Orna. Rather than live the double life of a mild-mannered reporter, Kal works at the Institute of Geology. And although he is loved by his family-of-choice, his family-of-origin is filled with turmoil.

In *Superman #53* "The Origins of Superman" (1948), Jor-El predicted Krypton would be destroyed and was not believed by the Science Council. Due to their ignorance, Krypton was destroyed. Moments before Krypton's destruction, Jor-El sent Kal to Earth to become Clark Kent and, eventually, Superman. However, in the alternate reality created by the Black Mercy, Jor-El's predictions are wrong. Due to his insistence that Krypton will be destroyed, Jor-El forces him to resign from the Science Council, making him bitter, distant, and wishing for the resurrection of an "Old Krypton."

As Superman fights the effects of the Black Mercy, the alternate reality he imagined to be perfection falls apart. His father's extremist views lead to Kara's (Supergirl's) brutal attack, leaving her hospitalized. Riots erupt throughout Krypton as Jor-El spouts hate speech from a pulpit. The alternate reality comes to an end with Kal and Van standing in the Kandor Crater as the world fades from existence, Batman removes the Black Mercy, and Superman regains consciousness.

Unlike *Superman #141*, Superman does not view Krypton through the eyes of a farmer boy raised in Kansas. Instead, he experiences what life would have been like as a Kryptonian with a father, wife, and children of his own, making the comic ideal to help understand why some male survivors of childhood sexual abuse cope using the Kal-El facade.

Developing the Kal-El Facade

What does it mean to be a man? Is it innate? Is each boy born with an understanding of how to achieve manhood, or is it learned implicitly and explicitly over time through conversations, actions, and interactions with friends, family, and numerous other factors? Although many individuals believe the former to be true, more individuals are coming to accept the latter as the truth. Rather than being born knowing what it means to be a "real man," boys learn the unwritten rules of manhood through socialization. To understand how boys are socialized into men over the progression of adolescence, there is no better example than Superman's development of the Kal-El identity. Although Superman is an alien from the planet Krypton, he was raised on Earth as a human. He did not know of his Kryptonian heritage until Jonathan and Martha Kent revealed the spaceship that crash-landed to Earth.

Superman's journey toward discovering his Kal-El identity is explained well in Geoff John's *Superman: Secret Origin*. In the comic, Jonathan Kent takes Clark into the cellar and reveals the spacecraft. Immediately, when Clark touched the smooth steel of the ship the image of his Kryptonian parents, Jor-El and Lara, appear. The hologram image of Jor-El and Lara explains Clark's unknown history when Jor-El says:

> You were not born on Earth, Kal-El. You were born on the planet Krypton. A world of great scientific achievement and adventure—but also a world of great tragedy. Krypton was a victim of its unstable red sun, but ultimately our fate was sealed because of my failure. I couldn't save Krypton, Kal-El—but I will save you. This sunstone crystal from the House of El contains everything I can give you after my death. You were sent here with a reason, Kal-El. You will be protected on this new world by the abilities its environment will provide you. And you will be free to move among the people of Earth. But never forget, although you look like one of them, you are not one of them.

With these words, Clark's eyes glow red with heat vision as tears steam from the creases of his eyes just before he attempts to destroy the ship and the hologram of his birth parents. It is in this moment that Clark's Kal-El identity is born. Clark discovers he is different in a way that others cannot see, but he can feel. The difference Clark feels inside after Jor-El says, "you are not one of them," is the same way male survivors believe they are different following the trauma of sexual abuse. Unlike Clark, male survivors have to learn the rules of being a "real" man through the socialization of the "boy code."

The Boy Code and the Birth of the Kal-El Facade

Some male survivors who portray the Kal-El facade to cope with the trauma of being sexually abused can sometimes appear hypermasculine. Many believe sexual abuse and assault is about sex, but it is not. Instead, sexual abuse and assault is about stripping an individual of their power and strength in an attempt for the perpetrator to regain a sense of control of their own life. Some male survivors who have been sexually assaulted attempt to regain the sense of control that was stripped away by projecting an image of being "man enough" or like a "real man" in an attempt to no longer feel the same weakness and lack of control that was experienced following the trauma of being sexually abused.

Male survivors who portray the Kal-El facade also follow the boy code. Rather than the good-guy code of the Clark Kent facade, where male survivors attempt to feel safe by appeasing their abuser and others around them, or the hero code of the Superman facade, were survivors attempt to regain strength by rescuing others, the boy code follows an alternate set of rules.

Similar to the hero code, boys are socialized from a young age to follow the boy code, described by William S. Pollack, associate clinical professor of psychology at Harvard Medical School, and author of *Real Boys: Rescuing Our Sons from the Myths of Boyhood*, as:

The sturdy oak: Men should be stoic, independent, and refrain from showing weakness.

Give 'em hell: Boys and men should be macho, take risks, and use violence.

The big wheel: Men should demonstrate their power and dominance and how they've got everything under control, even when they don't.

No sissy stuff: Real men don't cry or display emotions that might be viewed as feminine; doing so leaves men open to being labeled as "sissies" or "fags."

The indoctrination of these stereotypes at such a young age leads men to suffer in silence and self-medicate with drugs and alcohol abuse rather than seek help through counseling or therapy. The boy code perpetuates the belief that boys should learn to hold in their emotions, deal with them personally, and that given enough time they will go away. These beliefs lead to alcohol and other substance-related disorders, sleep disorders, pyromania, intermittent explosive disorder, pathological gambling, and sexual disorders such as exhibitionism, pedophilia, and voyeurism, according to the Prevention Institute (2014).

Similar to Clark, male survivors believe the truth of who they are must remain a secret, hidden from the rest of the world in order to fit in. While Clark uses the sunstone crystal to understand what it means to embody the heritage of Krypton as Kal-El, male survivors use the words and actions of others to understand how to fulfill society's definition of what it means to be a "real man" and "man enough." Although both Kal-El and male survivors attempt to fulfill false stereotypes to fit in, both feel alienated and alone as they struggle to comprehend their conflicting thoughts, actions, and emotions that they believe must be stifled to survive.

The Kal-El Facade and Dialectical Behavior Therapy

One form of the therapy that aligns with the Kal-El facade is **Dialectical Behavior Therapy (DBT)**. Unlike the *unbounded boundaries* of the Clark Kent facade, or the *rigid boundaries* of the Superman facade, survivors of the Kal-El facade alternate between an unbounded and a rigid boundary. In the same way Superman attempts to manage his humanity as Clark Kent and fear of having limitless power in a fragile world as Superman, Kal-El attempts to honor the Kryptonian heritage he feels obligated to remember because of its destruction and in being one of the planet's sole survivors.

Males who cope with the trauma of childhood sexual abuse using the Kal-El facade battle with feeling man enough. This means sometimes identifying with the Clark Kent facade's ability to avoid the feeling of overwhelming emotions. Unfortunately, these survivors may also view themselves and their actions as those of their perpetrator, which makes them feel shameful. To no longer view themselves as a villain, male survivors cope by assuming the Clark Kent facade. These male survivors mind read, people please, and place the needs and wants of others above their own. When these survivors become triggered, the Kal-El facade shifts from the Clark Kent facade, replacing people pleasing behavior with a belief that they are not being man enough. The good-guy code of the Clark Kent facade violates the Kal-El facade teachings of the boy code. When this occurs, the boundaries of the survivor shift from unbounded to rigid (Clark Kent into Superman), making the survivor withdraw from relationships in an attempt to conceal emotions. Unfortunately, when male survivors believe their boundaries are too rigid, the Clark Kent facade assumes control, transforming the hero code into the good-guy code, and perpetuating the cycle of living a life behind the mask of a facade. An example of the *wavering boundaries* of the Kal-El facade can be seen in the interaction between Kal-El's father, Jor-El, on the glass forest terrace of his housing complex in the alternate reality created by the Black Mercy.

In "For the Man Who Has Everything," discussed in the introduction to this chapter, Kal-El meets his father at his housing complex the day after his surprise birthday party. While there, Kal-El discovers that his father is participating in an extremist political organization called "Sword of Rao" in support of the Old Krypton Movement. In this alternate reality, Jor-El is no longer a part of the Science Council of Krypton. Instead, he has been forced to resign his position on the council due to his false prediction that Krypton would be destroyed. The debunking of his theories as the ravings of a madman leave him angry and bitter. To cope, Jor-El projects his shortcomings on the current political and social downfall and the inabilities of his son to fulfill the expectations of what it means to be a real a Kryptonian. His frustration can be detected when he tells his son, "Look around you, Kal. What's happened to Krypton? There's the drug traffic in Glamor-Salts and Hellblossom coming in from Erkol. There's racial trouble with the Vathlo Islan immigrants."

Rather than remain rigid in his boundaries, Kal-El attempts to explain to his father that Krypton is changing and that extremist political groups are not helping. In response, Jor-El attacks his son's shortcomings as a real man when he says, "and grubbing for rocks in the Kandor Crater is, I suppose? I had great hopes for you, Kal." Kal-El does not fight with his father. Instead, he leaves, forcing his father to smash the glass figure of a mother bird feeding her young with his cane before standing alone, crying into his hands.

If this scene is viewed through the lens of **Dialectical Behavior Therapy**, Kal-El's words and actions represents the wavering boundaries of the Kal-El facade, while Jor-El's words and actions are the rigid boundaries of the Superman facade. Because the Black Mercy is a product of Superman's own thoughts and wishes, both Jor-El and Kal-El are extensions of Superman's own thoughts and beliefs. Jor-El's actions and words represent Superman's belief in the need for a rigid boy code. As a "sturdy oak," he refuses to show weakness, and as the "big wheel," he displays that everything is under control even when it is not. Similar to Jor-El, male survivors also attempt to appear having everything under control while bottling their emotions. Also, like Jor-El, a male survivor's refusal to demonstrate any "sissy stuff" results in an outburst of anger and an inability to show intimacy in the same way Jor-El destroys the glass bird and refuses to provide Kal with any words of praise.

The internal battle of Superman between Kal-El and Jor-El represents the internal verbal battle and outward portrayal of a male survivor's Kal-El facade. Similar to Kal-El, male survivors feel attacked and less of a man internally, but outwardly they portray the behavior and words of Jor-El. They become passive-aggressive, angry, and violent. It is a battle that wavers from one facade to the other as the internal battle ensues. The Kal-El facade in relation to the survivor and the other facades can be viewed through the lens of DBT and **Internal Family System Therapy (IFS)** as well.

Internal Family Systems Therapy and the Kal-El Facade

If the Kal-El facade is viewed through the lens of **IFS therapy**, the Clark Kent facade is the *exile* portion of the self. The Clark Kent facade carries the burden and shame of being a male survivor of sexual abuse in the same way Clark Kent carries the shame of being different from others as an alien from another planet. To no longer carry these feelings of shame, the *firefighter* represses these emotions and beliefs by attempting to become man enough. In the case of Superman, this means being Kryptonian enough when he is criticized for behaving too human. For men, this equates to being labeled too emotional. To protect the Clark Kent facade (the exile) from the attacks of the Kal-El facade (the firefighter) for being too weak or too human, the Superman facade acts as the *manager* attempting to protect the Clark Kent facade.

This internal conflict between the exile, the firefighter, and the manager of a male survivor's psyche can be better understood by returning to the comic "For the Man Who Has Everything" discussed in the introduction of this chapter. In the comic, Superman depicts the same internal struggle that male survivors of childhood sexual abuse experience when the Black Mercy is removed from Superman's chest and the alternate reality comes to an end. As Superman (the manager) fights the effects of the Black Mercy to end the alternate reality, Kal-El (the firefighter) attempts to remain a Kryptonian as he fights to keep his son Van-El from vanishing from existence. The Superman facade fights the Kal-El facade and the alternate reality of the Black Mercy to save the Clark Kent facade in the same way male survivors battle thoughts and actions requiring the need to be man enough.

Male survivors who cope with the Kal-El facade consistently feel the need to be "enough." This is especially true for male survivors of different ethnicities and cultures. On top of the need to display what it means to be a real man, these male survivors have the compounding requirement to be "black enough," "Hispanic enough," "Asian enough," etc. The requirement to live up to false definitions of manhood strengthens the Kal-El facade, suppresses the survivor's emotions, and makes them feel further isolated from friends, family, and loved ones.

Chapter Ten: Consequences of the Kal-El Facade

"Every day I desperately try to live up to what everyone expects from me."

Superman—*Superman #2* (2018), "The Unity Saga: Part 6"

Male survivors who cope with the trauma of childhood sexual abuse with the Kal-El facade have difficulty believing they are enough. The Kal-El facade makes them believe they can always do more. Always be more. That their efforts are never enough because they are not truly man enough. The Kal-El facade makes the survivor believe they are damaged beyond repair and that this weakness makes them less of a man. To compensate they become hypermasculine to prove to others (and to themselves) that they are man enough.

Unfortunately, male survivors believe they have fallen short of achieving the pinnacle of manhood following childhood sexual abuse. Rather than believing they can mature into becoming a good man, male survivors believe the perfection of manhood can only be achieved through the Kal-El facade of being a real man and living by the boy code. However, perfection is never a possibility with the Kal-El facade. This is because of the push-and-pull that the Kal-El facade experiences as it attempts to live by the standards of different worlds. This is especially true for male survivors who are also minorities. While attempting to be man enough, minority male survivors also attempt to be enough for their own ethnicity.

Male survivors who have coped with the trauma of childhood sexual abuse using the Kal-El facade constantly feel a pull between needing to prove they represent what it means to be real men who live by the rules of the boy code while attempting to also be a good man who guides and mentors others. The belief in the need to live by the rules of the boy code and the trauma of being sexually abused creates a consistent feeling that they are different from other boys and men, from "real men." This experience can best be illustrated using Superman, the villain Brainiac, Jonathan Kent, and the bottled Kryptonian city of Kandor.

Brainiac, Kal-El, and Being Man Enough

In *Superman* #53 "The Origin of Superman" (1948), Jerry Siegel and Joe Shuster explain how the planet Krypton was destroyed after Kal-El's birth, and although his father, Jor-El, sent his only son to Earth in a spaceship, Kal-El is not the only living Kryptonian. In fact, until recently, there is an entire city of Kryptonians miniaturized and unable to grow to full size, but with their Kryptonian culture intact.

In *Superman* #242 "The Super-Duel in Space" (1958), Superman discovers an intact Kryptonian city aboard the spaceship of the alien villain Brainiac. Superman discovers that before Krypton's destruction, Brainiac miniaturized and bottled the Kryptonian capital, Kandor. When this occurred, all the people in the city were saved but forced to live life inside a glass bottle. This push and pull between needing to be a real Kryptonian and a human can be seen in Superman's thoughts as he tries to decide whether to enlarge the city of Kandor or himself:

Only one charge of hyper-forces left . . . enough to restore the Krypton city to normal size or me, but not both! Well, I'm only one man! The hyper-ray can save a million people in the Kryptonian city, allowing them to live on Earth! I'll press the button that will liberate them!

Unfortunately, before Superman can press the button, a miniaturized spaceship presses the button to enlarge Superman rather than Kandor. In this scene, Superman recognizes his

Kryptonian heritage but is pulled toward the life he has lived on Earth. Superman does not want to give up his own life but is willing to if it means becoming and being recognized as a "real Kryptonian." Male survivors are pulled toward similar self-destructive behavior such as keeping their emotions hidden, feigning confidence, and becoming hyperaggressive to live up to the societal standards of what it means to be a real man.

The push and pull of the Kal-El facade and the Clark Kent facade can further be seen in Geoff Johns' *Superman: Brainiac* (2009). In this graphic novel, Superman encounters Brainiac again and is consistently questioned (and being caused to question) his Kryptonian heritage, his humanity, and which is more important.

In numerous sections of the book, Superman calls into question whether he is Kryptonian or human. For example, when Kara (Supergirl and Superman's cousin) discovers Brainiac has returned, she is filled with fear as she relives memories of losing her parents on Krypton. She looks up at Superman with tears in her eyes: "Sometimes, I wish I didn't have any memories of Krypton. Maybe then I'd be like you. Maybe then I wouldn't miss it so much." Afterward, Superman holds her with an expression of remorse along with pain that she does not view him as a true Kryptonian, like herself.

A similar circumstance occurs when Superman battles Brainiac on his alien ship. He calls Superman's devotion to his Kryptonian heritage into question when he says:

> Physically, you are Kryptonian. But within your limited cranial capacity, you consider yourself human, don't you? You are a being born of an amalgam of worlds. As am I. I am connected to every living being in my bio-shell. But I would never consider myself anything but Coluan. I would never betray my race as you have.

Although there is no truth to Brainiac's words, Superman believes he is right. This is because the superhero was born Kal-El, raised Clark Kent, and eventually becomes Superman. All of these factors compound on one another, making him believe he has violated his Kryptonian identity. Similar to the transformation of Clark's character into Superman, male survivors are born male, raised to live by the boy code, but following the trauma of being sexual abused, the Kal-El facade transforms survivors into facades of real men. Without healing, male survivors become characters living behind the mask of the Kal-El facade, attempting to exhibit their manhood through hypermasculinity. There is a pull to be seen as a real man rather than live as a good man. In the same way, Superman is pulled toward needing to show that he is a real Kryptonian in Michael Bendis' *Superman #2*.

Real Men, Superman, and General Zod

Male survivors often do not believe they are man enough. The impact of being sexually abused makes them feel like less of a man if the abuse or assault was committed by another male, or they feel shame if the assault was by a woman. To combat these feelings and beliefs of not being "man enough," male survivors of the Kal-El facade become hypermasculine to prove to themselves and others that they are a man. Superman attempts to prove his Kryptonian allegiance in *Superman #2*, "Unity Saga: Part 6" (2019) to General Zod while battling the villain Rogol Zaar.

In the Unity Saga, writer Michael Bendis turns the mythos of Superman on its head. Rather than Brainiac being the destroyer of Krypton, Bendis makes the destroyer of Superman's planet a villain name Rogol Zaar, a monstrous-looking being with different colored eyes and a staff capable of destroying a planet's core. In the series (and the prequel series *Man of Steel*), Zaar pledges to rid the galaxy of all Kryptonians. He proves his determination to follow through on his vow when he breaks into the Fortress of Solitude, destroys the bottled city of Kandor, and kills its inhabitants.

Afterward, in *Superman #2*, Superman and fellow Kryptonian, General Zod battle Rogol Zaar in the alternate dimension of the Phantom Zone. Throughout this battle, Superman second-guesses his lifelong pursuit to preserve life at all cost. While in superspeed, he thinks to himself:

Every day I desperately try to live up to what everyone expects from me. Which is what I want from me as well. But I'm not a child . . . But with only a split second to act and all these facts and feelings crashing around in my head—all I keep thinking, over and over, is no matter what he says he did to Krypton, or what he says it had to do with my father—whatever else this monster may or may not have done—I know one horrible sin that he must own. One terrible moment that I will now carry with me for the rest of my days. And I need him to hear me. Those words I've said only to Kara, Bruce, and Diana, "For Kandor!"

Afterward, Superman explains:

That wasn't for Rogol, that was for Zod. As soon as I opened my mouth I realized the only person who really needed to hear that was Zod. Even though I hold Zod in the same disregard as Rogol, I must have subconsciously just decided that I want Zod to unleash his hell.

Although the words and actions of Superman are those of a fictional character, they reveal how many males who portray the Kal-El facade may feel and what they may believe. Superman wants Zod to view him as a true Kryptonian, rather than a weakling who was raised to be weak by alien parents. Because Zod was born, raised, and defended Krypton as a soldier, he views Superman as ignorant of Kryptonian heritage and a betrayer of its people for putting humanity's needs before those of Krypton. Superman's scream, "For Kandor!" is a desperate wish to be recognized as a real Kryptonian and to hide his differences from Zod. The same can be said for male survivors of childhood sexual abuse. Male survivors who mask their emotions behind the Kal-El facade do not always live and behave by the boy code. Instead, they wear a facade to show that they are not different. They want other men to view them as one of the guys and a real man, rather than a deviant deserving of being ostracized. Acceptance by other men and boys who are viewed by society as portraying manliness helps to eliminate the shame associated with being a male survivor and believing they are different.

Although Superman views Zod as his enemy, Zod is still viewed as the pinnacle definition of what it means to be a Kryptonian. Zod's belief that Superman is less than Kryptonian can be seen in his words to Clark Kent in Geoff Johns' *Superman: Last Son of Krypton*. After escaping the Phantom Zone, he says:

Hello Kal-El, Superman, or should I call you Clark Kent? We have obtained glimpses into your life on this primitive planet for decades, and yet I have never understood your motives for self-degradation. Your father would be disgraced to discover you masquerading as one of these sub-Kryptonians. You've embraced their culture and abandoned your own.

Male survivors view themselves the same way General Zod views Superman, especially if they were sexually assaulted by a woman who is viewed as attractive by societal standards. It is a belief perpetuated by the boy code that heterosexual boys and men always want sex and are always in search of their next opportunity to get laid. Those boys and men who are not are seen as not real men or as having something wrong with them that needs fixing. Male survivors believe that if they did not want the sexual advances, they have broken the boy code and are not real men in the same way Zod views Superman as sub-Kryptonian rather than the Kryptonian survivor, Kal-El. The only way to eliminate these feelings of shame is through healing and association, rather than dissociation, of the Kal-El facade into the self.

Chapter Eleven: Conquering the Kal-El Facade

"For Kandor!"

Superman—*Superman #2* (2018), "The Unity Saga: Part 6"

Healing the Kal-El facade means breaking the boy code and beginning the process of learning to feel and manage emotions properly. A way to accomplish this task is with the subjective **units of distress scale (SUDS)**. The structure of the scale is similar to the SUDS scale in "Part One: The Clark Kent Facade." However, this scale has been modified for survivors of complex PTSD to assist in leading them from feelings of numbness when at a ranking of *zero* to *four* on the SUDS scale, or from feeling of extreme rage when at a ranking from *six* to *ten*, to a safe regulation of emotions when at a ranking of *five*. The goal is not to achieve a feeling of numbness with a ranking of zero or a cascade of paralyzing emotions ranging from rage to distress and shame with a ranking of ten. Instead, the goal is to feel emotions but be able to manage and express them in a healthy manner with a ranking of *four*, *five*, or *six*. Reaching one of these three rankings takes time, practice, and putting in the work to recognize negative automatic thoughts with **Cognitive Behavior Therapy** in order to change them into true statements that are neither positive nor negative.

To use this chart, we need to understand Kryptonite and its effects on Superman. Although Superman was born Kal-El on the planet Krypton, he gets his super abilities from the Earth's yellow sun. Radiation contained in the material from his home planet of Krypton has the ability to harm the superhero.

Subjective Units of Distress Scale (SUDS)

Numeric Rating	Description
Zero: Green Kryptonite	A zero on the SUDS scale is similar to Superman being exposed to so much green kryptonite over such a long period of time that he is drained of all his power and dies. In Jerry Siegel's 1968 classic "The Death of Superman," Lex Luthor does just that to Superman. Being at a zero on the SUDS scale is similar. Green kryptonite has the ability to physically harm Superman, stripping the hero of his super abilities. Being around the green meteorite makes him feel sick, nauseous, and it causes physical pain as it drains him of his powers. When the kryptonite is taken away, the pain dissipates and Superman's powers eventually return. However, prolonged exposure to green kryptonite has the ability to kill the superhero. If you, as a male survivor, are at a zero, your ability to feel and express emotion has been drained over time due to the duration of your abuse. The prolonged physical and psychological pain of being sexually abused makes you feel as though your emotions are dead in the same way prolonged exposure to green kryptonite has the potential to kill Superman. At zero, you have become numb to feeling emotions. The impact of your childhood trauma and the bombardment of overwhelming experiences causes you to dissociate from feeling any emotion and to no longer feel pain due to the impact of your childhood trauma.
One: Red Kryptonite	A one on the SUDS scale is similar to red kryptonite's effect on Superman. Unlike green

	kryptonite, the impact of red kryptonite is different on Superman each time he is exposed to the meteorite. However, a consistency of red kryptonite is that it removes Superman's inhibitions, making him behave in a way that is rebellious and self-centered. As a male survivor, if you are at a one on this scale, you may be close to becoming numb to emotions and not care about the results of your actions in the same way Superman's feeling of intoxication can cause him to become reckless, angry, irritated, and sometimes over-sexualized. This is because of growing frustration at the lack of control the survivor has over their life.
Two: Silver Kryptonite	A two on the SUDS scale is similar to silver kryptonite's effect on Superman. Similar to red kryptonite, silver kryptonite hinders Superman's inhibitions. However, unlike red kryptonite, silver kryptonite makes Superman appear as if he is intoxicated by alcohol or marijuana. As a male survivor at a two on the SUDS scale, you appear to be carefree and concerned only with having a good time. This is because of a need to distance yourself from your emotions and limit their effects. Not because you do not care, but because you have learned that feeling emotions only leads to unbearable pain.
Three: Black Kryptonite	A three on the SUDS scale is similar to one of the effects of black kryptonite on Superman. Black kryptonite splits the personality of Superman in two. One which is good, and one which is evil. When at a three on the SUDS scale, you, as a male survivor, embrace the emotions that are considered to be those of a people pleaser. Although it may appear

	that ridding yourself of all evil would heal your childhood trauma and keep you from venturing down the path of becoming an abuser, it creates loosely defined boundaries that allow others to prioritize their own interests before your own. These loose boundaries cause you, as a male survivor, to ignore your own feelings and to put the needs and wants of others before your own. This eliminates feelings of shame associated with your childhood trauma.
Four: Gold Kryptonite (Post *Crisis on Infinite Earths)*	A four on the SUDS scale is similar to Superman being exposed to the gold kryptonite of post *Crisis on Infinite Earths.* Superman's superhuman abilities allow him to be impenetrable to physical harm, but his heightened senses cause him to remain hyper-aware at all times. While he is impenetrable to physical harm, he never receives a moment of rest due to his ability to hear and see things humans cannot. The trauma of being sexually abused can have the same effect on you as a male survivor. The impact of your abuse may cause trauma in a way that you become numb to pain in the same way Superman is not affected by the impact of a bullet on his skin. However, the goal is not to become numb to emotions and not feel pain, but to manage emotions and thoughts in a way that is healthy and not hyper-aware. Your goal is to feel and manage emotions like Superman when exposed to gold kryptonite. This is what it means to be at a four on the SUDS scale. However, like the effects of gold kryptonite in the comic book *Crisis on Infinite Earths*, the ability to manage your emotions and allow yourself to feel is not permanent. It wavers in

	and out. The goal is to reach a five on the SUDS scale, feel emotions, and have the ability to self-regulate good and bad feelings.
Five: <u>Gold Kryptonite</u> (*Pre-Crisis on Infinite Earths*)	A five on the SUDS scale is similar to Superman being exposed to gold kryptonite, but the gold kryptonite of pre-*Crisis on Infinite Earths*. In Alan Moore's *What Ever Happened to the Man of Tomorrow*, it is revealed to the world on national television by the villain, Toy Man, that Clark Kent and Superman are the same person, forcing the superhero to rid himself of his Clark Kent facade. Later, Superman breaks his law to never kill when he sees no other option than to kill Mr. Mxyzptlk and save the life of Lois and himself. This violation of his "Superman code" leads to the destruction of his Superman facade. Afterward, he walks into a room of gold kryptonite and walks out into the barren tundra of the North Pole to die and destroy the final facade of Kal-El. It is not revealed until the end that Superman did not die but instead became human, married Lois Lane, and began a family of his own free of any facade, becoming a complete person. This is your goal as a male survivor and what is achieved when reaching a five on the SUDS scale. In comics created before *Crisis on Infinite Earths*, gold kryptonite's effects were permanent for the Man of Tomorrow. Achieving a five on the SUDS scale means feeling a range of emotions while having the ability to not let them overwhelm you. It means feeling human and having the ability to manage your emotions without feeling impenetrable to emotion in the same way Superman is impenetrable to physical harm or

	having emotions which are hypersensitive in the same manner as Superman's superhuman abilities.
Six: Gold Kryptonite (Post Crisis on Infinite Earths)	A six on the SUDS scale is similar to Superman being exposed to the gold kryptonite of post *Crisis on Infinite Earths,* however in a slightly different manner than discussed previously. In Alan Moore's "The Jungle Line," Superman becomes infected with a bloodmorel from the planet Krypton. This disease causes his powers to fade in and out without warning. Superman experiences moments of torture when his super abilities awaken without warning, causing his senses to become bombarded by the sounds and smells of day-to-day life. Other times his super abilities fade, causing him to be shocked at the sight of his own blood from a papercut. Later, Superman becomes so angry as he fights for his survival that he destroys an entire forest as the antihero Swamp Thing attempts to calm him down. This is what it is like to be a six on the SUDS scale. Similar to being a four on the SUDS scale, feeling as if you are a six means no longer feeling numb to emotion, but instead being hypersensitive to your feelings, causing them to overwhelm you to the point of losing control. While you may be able to manage the hypersensitivity of emotions occasionally in the same manner as Superman when he feels human when exposed to gold kryptonite, the goal is to always feel human and have control over your emotions while allowing yourself to feel them without regret and shame.
Seven: Black Kryptonite	A seven on the SUDS scale is similar to the effects of black kryptonite on Superman. Unlike a three on the SUDS scale, black kryptonite has the effect of

	splitting Superman into his evil counterpart. Like Superman, the emotions you feel bombard you with sadness, anger, and resentment for others and yourself. Similar to Superman when exposed to black kryptonite, the evil portion of yourself blames others for your actions, rather than hold yourself accountable. Merging the two halves of the self will help in reaching a five on the SUDS scale.
Eight: Parasite	An eight on the SUDS scale is similar to being attacked and sucked dry of all your energy by the villain Parasite. Parasite's origin begins with a janitor, Rudy Jones. There are different backstories to how Rudy became Parasite, but in most he is exposed to a toxic chemical from Lexcorp and gains the ability to absorb the lifeforce from living creatures by either touching their skin or latching himself to their flesh with razor-sharp teeth. Parasite is not only able to absorb the lifeforce of humans and animals, but Superman as well. Parasite drains Superman of his power to the point where Superman feels exhausted and unable to function. This is what it feels like for you, as a male survivor of childhood sexual abuse, to be at an eight on the SUDS scale. You believe you feel emotions too deeply, causing you to be overwhelmed by anger, frustration, and anxiety to the point of exhaustion, draining your lifeforce in the same way Parasite drains the lifeforce of Superman.
Nine: Magic	A nine on the SUDS scale is similar to Superman being attacked by a villain who has the ability to wield magic. Other than kryptonite, magic is one of the few other substances in the DC universe that can harm Superman. Unlike green kryptonite, magic has

	not been known to kill Superman but does severely harm him. If you, as a male survivor of childhood sexual abuse, are at a nine on the SUDS scale, your emotions overwhelm you to the point of physical pain in the same way Superman is harmed when exposed to magic. To feel emotions physically hurts, and you wish they would go away.
Ten: <u>Blue Kryptonite</u>	A ten on the SUDS scale is similar to blue kryptonite's effect on Bizarro Superman. Blue kryptonite does not have an effect on the real Superman. However, similar to green kryptonite on Superman, blue kryptonite has the potential to kill Bizarro. Unlike green kryptonite, blue kryptonite does not drain Bizarro of life. Instead, it does the exact opposite and overwhelms Bizarro with so much energy he explodes. This is similar to the way your emotions, as a male survivor of childhood sexual abuse, make you feel. Rather than feel drained of life after prolonged exposure to green kryptonite, your emotions overwhelm you to the point of explosive anger, anxiety, shame, and guilt in the same way blue kryptonite overwhelms Bizarro to the point of explosion.

Chapter Twelve: Conquering My Kal-El façade (Autobiographical)

"I can't help but think that with everything we've been through lately . . . and everything we know is coming . . . I'm saying: Maybe Superman is a luxury that we can't afford anymore."

Superman—*Superman #17* (2019), "The Truth: Prologue"

The key to conquering the Kal-El facade is creating a narrative that is true to the sexual abuse you remember, rather than honoring the rules of the boy code. There is no way to guide you through creating a personal narrative. It is a truth that only you as a male survivor of childhood sexual abuse know to be true. Judith Herman explains this line of reasoning in her book *Trauma and Recovery* when she explains how survivors of sexual abuse are survivors of a war in which they are the only soldier. This means that although you create a narrative, it does not have to be anyone else's truth except your own.

The truth survivors should seek when writing a narrative is not in the form of seeking justice from the law but in understanding the abuse *you* remember taking place as a child. The narrative may be incomplete or disjointed, and that is okay. It is meant to be built and added to over time as more memories surface throughout the healing process. Not only is a sexual abuse survivor the sole survivor of a war they must fight alone, trauma of sexual abuse also affects the functionality of the brain, transforming how thoughts form, making it difficult (sometimes impossible) to remember all the traumatic abuse events. The isolation male survivors experience when forming their narrative is exacerbated if the only other person who knows the abuse occurred is the abuser. This person may not admit that the abuse or assault ever occurred or may reveal only half-truths about the abuse. The perpetrator of the sexual abuse may no longer be alive to verify the abuse ever took place. All of these factors make creating a comprehensive narrative sometimes nearly impossible, but that does not diminish the necessity of the exercise.

Writing a narrative provides a way of knowing the abuse occurred and an ability to acknowledge that it affected you. It is a powerful tool that helps provide you with a voice that may have been stifled for much of your young and adult life.

Below is the narrative of my own abuse that first appeared in *Raped Black Male: A Memoir*. Since then I have added to my narrative in *How to Kill Your Batman*.

Men Can't Be Raped (from *Raped Black Male: A Memoir*)

I wish I had a better memory of what occurred the first time I was raped, but it's been twenty years, and some of the memories have become hazy. I do know the house was empty of my parents and brother. What's interesting is that the first time wasn't the first time. It began with my abuser and a pornographic videotape. My abuser was my sister, who at the time was also my babysitter. I would often have a babysitter when Mom had to work late at Kmart or Dad went out and had to DJ at the American Legion. My parents also simply went out sometimes (as parents should), or they did not get home from work until 5 p.m. So, during that time when my sister and I were alone is when the grooming began.

Grooming is not what you may think. It is not when two individuals sit down and brush and comb each other's hair like chimps in a zoo. Grooming is a term used to explain how abusers prepare their victims for molestation. For some abusers, it occurs when the victim runs around, becoming excited while playing tag, for example. Then, instead of continuing the game, the abuser grabs the genitals or breasts of his/her victim—anything to get the child sexually aroused and excited while making the victim believe he/she is safe and participating in a fun game. Afterward, the roles are reversed. The abuser has the victim run, tag, and touch him / her in the same way. This makes the victim believe this is how the game is played and allows the abuser to open the door to more egregious acts and games in which the abuser can easily sexually assault with less resistance and more severity.

My grooming occurred in the form of pornographic movies.

My dad had a collection of pornographic videocassettes under the mattress of the bed in our basement. They were easily accessible and could be returned as if they had never been touched. Eventually, after the basement had been remodeled and the bed and mattress were thrown into the trash, the cassettes were moved to the bottom drawer of a desk in the basement.

I remember this bed vividly. Me, my sister, and Daniel would often play on the mattress when my parents were gone. I would lie on the mattress while they ran and jumped on the bed to try and fling me into the air and against the wall. I loved it. It was crazy, stupid, innocent stuff kids do when their parents are gone, unlike what eventually happened when Daniel moved away after physically fighting with my father and my sister began sexually abusing me.

The grooming began one afternoon when my parents were gone. I was being babysat, and she asked with a calm, happy smile after entering my room, "Hey, Kenny, wanna see something cool?" Of course, I agreed. I was eight years old. I lived for cool. Cool was my life, and she knew it.

From my room she led me down to the basement, lifted the mattress, removed the black cassette tape, and placed it in the VCR. I remember that the cassette was not labeled as pornography; instead it had a normal white label on the spine of the cassette, as if it had once been a different movie that had been recorded over.

Because it looked so similar to many other movies in our library, I never suspected its contents.

The video had been paused in the middle of the cassette, so it did not start at the beginning. Instead, it continued from the last moment my father pressed the stop button, which was in the middle of two people moving, groaning, and humping in ways I had no idea was possible at such an age. Immediately I was disgusted. At the time, I did not know what it was, but I knew it was a movie I was not supposed to watch. My eight-year-old brain flashed back to scenes of Spike Lee's *School Daze* and my parents telling me to cover my eyes during the "dirty parts." Seeing what was happening on the screen, I figured this was most definitely a dirty part that I was not allowed to watch, so I covered my eyes and waited for the okay that the scene had ended and I could open my eyes to something safe. Instead, she took my hands from my eyes and said, "Watch. It's funny." I tried to cover my eyes during a few scenes that followed that were especially embarrassing, but I was coaxed into watching.

Soon it was over. When it came to the end, she rewound the cassette tape to where it began, put it back under the mattress, and went back upstairs to continue the day. Nothing happened. She did not try to touch me or tell me to touch her. Rather than grooming me to become sexually aroused through a game that allowed us to explore each other's bodies, she groomed me to like the idea of sex through the use of movies, which were a primary source of entertainment in our house. Any free moment the family had was spent watching movies. We all had our classic repeats that we could (and did) watch over and over again. My mother loved *Toy Soldiers, The Five Heartbeats,* and *The Temptations.* Daniel loved *The Last Dragon.* I loved *The Rocketeer* and *Hook.* My father loved movies in general. Going to Blockbuster on Friday evenings to search the shelves for a new release or an unwatched classic was our regular routine. Because movies were such a large part of my family's life, pornographic movies could be made to seem like a safe, fun, and common form of entertainment that my eight-year-old self would never question as being invalid and unacceptable. It was a way to groom me.

Of course, I knew not to tell anyone about watching the videos. My sister never told not to tell, but I knew. Technically, nothing happened, but I had been prepared after years of accidentally breaking figurines, rules of staying indoors, and going places that were off-limits after my parents had vacated the house—what happened while they were gone was not to be discussed, unless we were caught. It ensured that no one got in trouble. Unfortunately, my abuser never got caught.

For months, this is how it went: my parents would leave, she would get the tape from under the mattress, we would watch, put it back, and continue with our day, never saying a word to our parents. The only other person to tell who could have stopped the abuse from happening was Daniel, who was eighteen years old and living in Germany. After high school and attending Alabama A&M in Huntsville, Alabama, for a year, Daniel dropped out of college, joined the military, and moved to Germany to raise a family of his own.

Although the grooming lasted for a number of weeks, it eventually turned to something much more sinister. As time progressed and the grooming continued, my abuser and I no longer sat on the floor together watching the video in silence, in disgust, or in mock laughter. Instead, each of us had our own positions in the room, separate from the other. She lay on the bed with a comforter over her body while I sat on the couch and watched the scenes play out on the screen. After weeks of watching the cassette in secret on weekends or late at night when our parents were gone, I no longer covered my eyes and looked away in embarrassment. In fact, most times I had become sexually aroused. My therapist tells me that this is normal—a natural reaction of the body to the stimulation of the brain. But I find it hard not to view myself as a protagonist of the sex and abuse, no matter what she tells me. However, I did not masturbate, mostly because I had no idea what masturbation was or that it was even possible. I was too young to know. My abuser, on the other hand, being five years my senior, was discovering masturbation beneath the comforter on the mattress ten feet away, watching women receive pleasure from men in the same way she was sexually stimulating herself.

After being groomed to willingly watch pornography, remaining silent and sexually aroused while my sister was sexually stimulated through masturbation, all the pieces had fallen into place for me to be raped with little resistance, and that's precisely what occurred.

The first time in which grooming became rape, my abuser called me to the bed where she lay with the blanket pulled over her body. I looked at the bed and walked over. She said calmly but with hesitation, "Let's try something different. Get on top of me." This is when she pulled back the blanket to reveal she was wearing no pants or panties.

Immediately I froze. I had no idea what to say or do. I thought to myself, *Is this okay? Can I say no?*

I wanted to say no, but I didn't know how. How could I? She was someone I trusted. I thought I had to do what she said. She was my sister. I believed with all my heart, beyond the shadow of a doubt, that she wouldn't do anything to hurt me. It's taken nearly thirty years, therapy, and meditation for this belief to finally change.

In the moment, she noticed my hesitation and knew she couldn't give me an option. With more confidence—invitingly but with more force—she said, "Let's do what they do. Come on," as she worked off my pants.

When the rape happened and she placed me on top of her, I didn't move. I lay there, lifeless, uncomfortable, and cold. She was larger and there was no way for me to touch the mattress, so I lay hovering in the air on top and inside her body as the pornographic movie continued to play in the background. When I didn't move, she became frustrated and annoyed that I wasn't doing it right. Again, she took control over the situation, grabbed me by the waist and made me move up and down, in and out, as she watched the scenes play out on the screen on the other side of the room. It lasted only a few minutes, but the impact has yet to vanish. She finished, and I stopped moving. We both got dressed, she rewound the tape and put it back under the mattress as always. But this time was different. Rather than go upstairs to continue her day, she stopped and told me as she had never done before, "Don't tell. It's bad and we'll get in trouble."

I was too young to argue or know what it meant, so I didn't tell. I remained silent, just as she wanted. For over twenty years, I remained quiet because I didn't want to "get in trouble"; I thought it was my fault and I'd be punished. There was nothing I could do if I didn't want Mom, Dad, and Daniel to look at me with the shame and regret I felt. I had done something wrong that no one knew had occurred except her, so the best and only option was to keep quiet and keep her secret.

How did this make me feel?

In the moment, I felt dirty. I curled up inside myself, waiting for it to stop, and I haven't stopped waiting. I didn't say much. There was no kissing or fondling, just sex. And that's how it went for almost two years. Our parents would leave, pornography would play, I would be raped, and I wouldn't tell. Over time, I began to anticipate when it was going to happen, even look forward to it. My therapist says this is natural. She says it's normal to have been aroused and sexually stimulated. It's something the body does and something I couldn't control, but it still doesn't change how I feel— that it was my fault.

That I could have stopped it.

That I enjoyed it.

That I'm to blame and, no matter what I do, I'm damned beyond the reach of forgiveness.

Then, one day, abruptly, the rapes stopped. After church, she told me we couldn't do it anymore because it was wrong and that it never happened. I said okay, but my mind was racing. One thought after another came into my mind without stopping.

You did this to me, and now you're saying we can't do it anymore? And you're telling me it never happened? You're telling me it was wrong—how wrong was it? Why was it wrong? What's going to happen to me if someone finds out?

It wasn't until much later that I would find answers to these questions.

You may be wondering why these rapes abruptly came to an end. I have asked the same question. I believed for years that she had an epiphany, realizing that she was psychologically, physically, and morally damaging someone she was supposed to love and protect. But the truth is much more logical and hurtful. I had become too old and was no longer useful. In the two years since this all began, I had gone from an eight-year-old child to a ten-year-old prepubescent boy who could get my fifteen-year-old sister pregnant. Pregnancy meant being discovered, and this was something she could not allow to happen. So, instead, she told me it was wrong and brought it to an end, leaving me broken and confused, with no help to understand the incest that had occurred. She allowed the thought that would mature into a belief and eventually become a cold hard fact in my mind: men can't be raped.

Our culture and society implicitly communicates, through its celebration of hyper-masculinity and clichéd ideas of what it means to be a man, that rape is an impossible fate for a red-blooded, heterosexual male. There's no way you can be the victim of sexual assault, unless you are a woman or a homosexual. These beliefs, seen through the eyes of the warped and damaged ego of a perpetual eight-year-old, helped to create the negative view of myself I have today. A view I attempt to conquer once a week in therapy, like Quixote's ever shifting and fictional windmills.

Our society believes raping of males never occurs because the sexual abuse of males is hardly ever reported, no matter what the age. Therefore, it seemingly does not exist. Male survivors of sexual assault, meanwhile, suffer under the assumption that they're the only male to have been raped, leaving them feeling helpless, alone, damaged, and refusing to seek help. It leaves survivors like me feeling inadequate as men and human beings, with serious psychological consequences.

In no way am I asking for the spotlight to be taken from female rape survivors. However, when rape of a female does tragically occur, women usually know they are not alone. They know they're not the first, and, unfortunately, will not be the last. This does not rebuild the ego they were stripped of after being violated, but it can make seeking help more conceivable. Getting help is key to becoming healthy, and that is why I hope other male survivors read my story. Male survivors need to know they're not alone. They need to stop blaming themselves for what was done to them. They need to know that they did nothing wrong.

Rape is about power, control, and dominance—nothing else. It has nothing to do with sex. The abuse of male survivors is no different and neither was mine. To fully understand how this abuse was about power and control, you have to understand the history of my abuser and how it all began.

My abuser—my sister—was, like me, raped by her babysitter, Mr. Miller, probably around the same age that I was raped by her. When sexual abuse occurs at such a young age, the ability to feel safe and in control is stripped from the victim, leaving their psychological development stagnant between the ages of seven and nine. At this age, healthy individuals learn to gain independence, explore the world on their own, and take control of their environment. However, when an individual is raped at this age, such independence and control is stunted, leaving the child frozen in that early stage of psychological development. It is possible to progress through the other stages of development, but that stage will remain underdeveloped until help is sought and the wound can be healed properly. This means that without therapy and help, the rape victim will always feel as though they have no control over their life or their surroundings. This is why rape is powerful. It allows the abuser to seemingly take back some of the control that was taken from them, continuing the cycle and perpetuating more sexual assault and abuse until help is sought and the cycle is broken. This is what happened to my abuser.

At thirteen she was overweight, bullied, and felt as though she had lost all power in every aspect of her life. Being unable to seek help because of her embarrassment or fear of repercussions, she attempted to take back some control in the form of food—eating what she wanted, when she wanted. It was one of the few things that gave her pleasure and contentment. Unfortunately, gluttony was a bandage too small to deal with her psychological wound. The resulting obesity made her directionless, exposing her to bullying and rejection.

Her feelings of helplessness and powerlessness led her to sexually abuse me for a number of reasons. The primary reason was that I was the youngest. As the baby of the family, I could easily be groomed and manipulated into doing what she wanted. This also meant that she gained power through my weakness. Her dominance continues to this day and is one of the primary reasons that we no longer speak. By raping me, she stripped me of my ego, leaving me perpetually eight years old, seeking approval without the strength or ability to say no or to stand up for myself. Regaining my ego is what I struggle with in therapy. It wasn't until recently that I stopped sympathizing with my abuser and saw the years of rape for the vile acts they truly were.

Being the youngest of three also meant that I received the most attention. Generally, I was well-liked and accepted by my parents and brother. I was funny, happy, smart, and kind, while it seemed

155

she was none of the above. Seeing these qualities in me and not in herself may have ripped her to shreds inside. I was everything she wanted to be but physically and mentally could not be. So, she pulled me down. By raping me, she ensured I would always stay in my place and that she would always have the upper hand. It gave her the control over me that she always wanted over her own life. Years after the sexual assaults had come to an end, the mental abuse continued.

You may be wondering, was this planned? When she sat me down and put the VHS into the VCR, did she consciously intend to regain the control she had lost by taking mine? No, I don't believe so. Not then. However, now, I believe she does realize what she was doing. Throughout her adult life, she has sought to control, manipulate, and dominate every situation and relationship. Rather than seek help, she has continuously worsened over the years, and I fear for the mental health and stability of my nieces and nephew. Without help, her unstable personality will pass to her children through her words, actions, and behavior.

If rape and sexual abuse is all about power, dominance, and continuing the cycle, why haven't I become an abuser? Why am I not a sex offender? Honestly, there is no logical reason. According to my therapist, many people with my background are addicted to drugs; victims of alcohol abuse; struggling in education; and unable to sustain lasting, stable, and healthy relationships. Yet, I have never done a drug in my life (besides the 20 mg of Lexapro for my depression and anxiety), I drink no more than two beers before falling asleep. I have both a bachelor's degree from Bowling Green State University and a master's degree from Johns Hopkins University. I am a happy father and husband who could never dream of sleeping anywhere besides his own bed or the couch in my daughters' room if one of them were sick. There is no logical reason that I have patience or pleasure in working with some of the most annoying, frustrating, and coolest people on the planet— seventh graders. The only explanation is that I am truly blessed. My therapist believes that I have somehow been able to compartmentalize the abuse. She's not sure how, but I have a theory.

When I was younger, and even to this day, I loved superheroes. Then, and now, I adhered to what they stand for. In the realm of comic books, there was no gray; there was only black and white, right and wrong. I wanted to be on the side of light and good, and the only way I knew to do that was by trying to be perfect in every way. I could strive to be kind, intelligent, sympathetic, moral, and adhere to a code of honor. These beliefs about how to live and treat the people around me have stuck with me to this day. It's why I wrote my senior thesis on the evolution of chivalry through the ages—its representation and embodiment in knights, and the eventual replacement of knights by superheroes. This is the reason it took a year of therapy once a week before I stopped sympathizing with my abuser. In my mind, hating her was wrong because hate is wrong and because she was a relative. I believed she needed understanding until she found her way. However, my attitude toward her has changed. I know everyone is responsible for their own actions. And it is the thought of my nieces and nephew, writing these same words and going through these same struggles from a person who never received help because I remained silent, that pushed me to put my own story to paper.

I run, meditate, read, and go to church to not be the person / thing that I fear I will become. The cycle of abuse will not continue with me. But my abuser has made sure that I never get to know the eight-year-old boy that I have locked away in a room deep in the recesses of my mind.

Now (from *How to Kill Your Batman*)

Years have passed since the publication of *Raped Black Male: A Memoir.* Since then some things have changed, while others remain the same. In those four years I wish I could say I drink less, exercise more, and attend church each Sunday, but I can't. I'm still "two beers Rogers," resulting in a sleepy haze and goofiness that makes my wife giggle. Life has a way of becoming busier, pushing what once seemed a priority to the back burner, making room for true priorities such as family, friends, and writing as a source of support for others and myself.

I wish I could say life has become filled with less stress and anxiety over the years, and (in a way) I can. This is not because I have fixed all my problems and "healed" my childhood sexual abuse. In fact, it is just the opposite. Little has changed in the reality of my sexual abuse except the way I view life and approach problems. The last four years have been difficult, filled with heartbreaking loss when my son (Casus) passed away, and a deeper understanding of what it means to be a survivor for myself and others. Recovery is still a daily process. However, I can say I am happier and more at peace with the man I have become.

Most nights, nightmares plague my dreams, making me question reality from fiction when I awake, but fewer panic attacks result afterward. There are fewer mornings of sheer panic with my wife cradling me on the floor of our bathroom, telling me everything will be okay. There are fewer bouts of hypervigilant perfection in my own actions that make me feel shame and believe I am a failure who only deserves to die by my own hand. Each day I realize, more and more, that I am not perfect, but I continue to strive to become a better father, husband, educator, coach, mentor, guide, and survivor. Each day I fall short, but it does not stop me from waking up the next morning to try again.

Over time, more memories have returned about my sexual abuse. I can now see in my mind the pornographic VHS that was used and how the label read *The Little Mermaid*. This is possibly because my father ordered the pornographic video from Pay-Per-View, wanted to have the opportunity to watch it again at a later date, grabbed the first tape he could find, and recorded over the contents. The irony of the VHS *The Little Mermaid* holding the contents of a pornographic video titled *Roxanne* that resulted in the loss of my childhood innocence is not lost on me.

Memories of Peoria, my hometown, return as well. Memories of the fast-food restaurant Velvet Freeze across the street from where I would get onion rings and a hamburger that I bought with money from my paper route. Memories of the gas station on the corner, Landmark Cinema, the mall, Willow Knolls, and other memories that have nothing do with my sexual abuse but seemed to be pushed away and forgotten. I wish I knew why. Each causes me to pause and become lonely in a melancholy way when I remember times of happiness that were layered with depression, shame, and sadness.

I can now remember the layout of the basement (pre- and post-remodel) and how the small rectangle windows near the ceiling were used as an alert system when a shadow passed overhead, warning when a car had pulled into the driveway, or someone was walking to the back door. Eventually, I could remember seeing the black mildew and chipping paint of the wall below this window and remember how there was sometimes an unexplainable moisture that made the cement cool to the touch. In front of this wall is where the bed lay before the basement was remodeled. It was on this bed that I remember the videotape being hidden beneath the mattress, the pressure of her body on top of mine, and the odd odor on her breath that never seemed to go away no matter how often she brushed her teeth. I remember the darkness that room could hold and the smell of cigarettes that made it difficult to breathe when I sat close to my father's brown felt chair and the soda can filled with ash that was sometimes mistaken for Coke. At first, these memories haunted me without knowing why.

The weight of my pregnant wife while making love would make me feel depressed and dirty.

The smell of my daughter's breath in the morning before brushing her teeth would make me hate her.

The irrational fear of the larger preteen and teenage black girls I taught would make my heart feel as though it were going to burst from my chest when helping them to answer a simple question.

All of these factors would remind me of that basement and the fear I felt in that house on Wilson Dr. However, as my sister screamed at me one afternoon in a voicemail, this is only one side of the story. The bad side. And she was right.

Guilt (from *How to Kill Your Batman*)

In *Batman #25-32,* following the "War of Jokes and Riddles," Batman saw his actions as irredeemable when he attempted to stab the Riddler in the face with a machete to kill him. As Bruce Wayne, he recounts to Selina Kyle how, after the war, the world saw him as a hero. They gave him nicknames such as "The World's Greatest Detective" and "The Caped Crusader," but inside he felt as if he were living a lie.

While Bruce Wayne lives with feelings of guilt and shame for not being able to prevent the murder of his parents, these feelings of guilt and shame following the War of Jokes and Riddles were different. As a child, Bruce did not have the ability to stop the murder of his parents. However, Batman's attempts to kill the Riddler were actions *he* had control over. If the Joker (Yes! Joker!) had not stopped him, Batman would have crossed the line that separated himself from the criminals of Gotham City. The guilt he felt changed the way he saw himself and his actions. He no longer believed he was deserving of being loved by Selina, or anyone else.

These comics helped me to understand the guilt I felt after recounting the events of my childhood sexual abuse. It's a story where I am painted as the survivor and my sister as the abuser, but the answer is much more complex.

One morning, a few weeks after Thanksgiving, I woke up to a voicemail from my sister. For the longest time I was afraid to listen, terrified of what she would say. However, the fear of having an unanswered voicemail from her terrified me even more. With a racing heart, I pressed play and listened. She said, screaming into the phone:

I want to put this on the record. And this is your sister calling you. I just read the interview that you just gave and when I want to tell you that you did nothing but lie in that interview it's best with the fact that I chose not to get in contact with you. Kenny, you need to face your own shit too. I have sat back, not said anything, and I have let you put this book out there. And even in the event that this happened back at thirteen. And the fact that you acted as if nothing, nothing was wrong. And me and you even talked about this. And even in the fact now that I read this interview, and the way that you put me back out there, it is good where our relationship stands at because it was not by my choice; this was by your choice. And I will be taking screen shots and I will be sending this to Daddy and Mommy, and I will send it to anybody that needs to know because you are not the only one that has a voice in this situation. I do too. You use my situation in your book that was not given your permission to use by any means necessary.

I am so hurt by the way you doggin' me in this situation completely. I do not want to talk to you, and I do not want to hear back from you. But this is, and you can put this out so the world can hear this too. Because it seems like that's what you're choosing to do. You putting things out there, but yet, you don't remember the good things that's happened. And the way that I just read this interview. See, I'm glad (my husband) seen it for me until he just showed me this interview that you put me out there like this. Like this, Kenny? I mean, really? You put your sister out there like this? Oh my, God! After the shit I have done for you. As a young boy and as a man. This is how you treat me? This is how you repay back me? Like this? So, I hope you get this. And God have mercy on your soul, Kenny. Because this makes no sense at all! And the way you portray me out in this world as the woman that I am. And I been keeping my mouth shut and haven't said nothing to you. And then I let you go through your struggle, and letting you get help. This don't make no sense. So, this is personally from your sister. And it's (she was screaming and I could not understand what was said) *that you did not answer the phone because I am hurt! I am more hurt than anything, and they say healing starts first. And with you being a man know with the fact that you did! You don't know what the fuck I've been through! So, you need to get your damn interview and your damn story straight! And I mean it! And leave my name out your motherfucking mouth!*

After complaining to my therapist of chest pains after transcribing this message, she reminded me how stupid that was given my heart condition and convinced me to delete the message. However, the guilt I felt afterward remained. It was guilt I have felt for a long time, because it seemed I had betrayed my sister by telling only one half of the story. Not about the abuse, but afterward.

In high school, my mom and I were homeless during my junior and senior year. As a result of years of physical, verbal, and emotional abuse by my father, my parents went through a rough divorce, resulting in the foreclosure of our home and our living in the basement of the home of relatives. During those two years, and for a very long time before, I had been hurting. Rather than confront that pain, I became very hypervigilant. I focused on my schoolwork, sports, and extracurricular activities with the goal of getting to college. I believed that if I could get to college and escape, I would be healed. I could start *my* life and forget the past. Unfortunately, I was wrong.

By the time I graduated from Peoria High School, I received a full academic scholarship to Bowling Green State University. However, within a week of moving on campus I had become severely depressed. My days were spent in bed with severe stomach pain, crying, and confused about what was wrong with me. I know now how trauma affects the mind, body, and brain. The pain in my stomach was due to the vagus nerve becoming triggered and being faced with the realities of my past while living in new surroundings. When upset or feeling threatened, the vagus nerve becomes activated. It runs from the base of the skull, through the body, and ends at the colon. When threatened, the vagus nerve dries out the throat, increases the heart rate, causes gut-wrenching pain, and speeds up or slows down breathing. Because I ignored the complex trauma of being sexually abused as a child, living in an unstable household for all of my young adult life, and living in the basement of relatives for two years while attempting to excel in school to make it to college, my fight-or-flight mechanism kicked into overdrive, forcing the vagus never to cause gut-wrenching pains in my stomach. Later, this nerve and the complex PTSD of my past would be retriggered when a former Baltimore principal told me I was not allowed to state that I was a survivor of childhood sexual abuse while on school grounds, causing me to suffer from a viral heart infection from the stressful working conditions.

Within a week, I had withdrawn from my classes at BGSU, forfeiting my scholarship for the academic year. When I withdrew from my classes, I could not return to Peoria. The stress of not having a home was too much. Instead, I spent the year with my sister in Maryland, working at Old Navy and attempting to figure out my life. Eventually, I returned to BGSU, and after a semester of academic probation my scholarship was reinstated. However, I never returned back to Peoria during my breaks from school. If I did not stay on campus, I returned to Maryland to stay with my sister. She was there for me when I needed to recenter myself. And no matter what happened in the past, she is still my sister. While there are memories that are painful, she was right. There were good memories as well. Telling my story of sexual abuse made me feel as if I were the villain, playing the role of the hero. Unfortunately, life is not a comic of contained panels and black-and-white images. The realities of life were much more complex, and I did not know what that meant when first speaking of my abuse. Over the years, I have attempted to make sense of the relationship I did have with my sister and to figure out if there are any villains to this story and whether I am one of them.

I wish I knew the answer, but I don't. Heroes and villains are meant for comics and movies. Reality is more complex. However, I do know Batman carries the guilt of his actions in "The War of Jokes and Riddles," and that's okay. His guilt does not stop him from doing the right thing and holding himself accountable. He was wrong and would have had to pay a price if the Joker had not stopped him. Similar to Batman, I have to carry the guilt of telling the story of my abuse in which my sister raped me from ages eight to ten. This is not about being hypervigilant, this is about knowing that speaking of my abuse is the right thing to do. Telling my truth is not meant to harm her or my family. It has very little to do with any of them. It is about healing myself and letting other survivors know they are not alone.

I know the story of the relationship I have with my sister is complex, but while it requires a complex response, it also requires my sister to get the help she needs to heal if she would like to be a part of my life. Help I cannot give her. She helped save my life when I needed it the most. She stuck her hand in the way of the machete and stopped me from spiraling out of control. Unlike the relationship of the Joker and Batman, I carry fond memories of us sitting together in the cold of the car delivering newspapers; laughing and playing together with my nieces when I returned for summer break from college; and spending nights telling jokes to (and about) one another while watching old movies from our childhood. While some memories are pleasant, these times of happiness do not erase her past abuse. I do not blame her, but I do, and will, hold her accountable. I love her. Always will. It's for this reason my door will always be open when she makes the decision to heal and begin the process of recovery. Until then . . .

Privilege

In the blink of an eye, planet Krypton's heritage, culture, and history were wiped from existence with an explosion that was absorbed by the vacuum of space. When Jor-El and Lara learn of their planet's imminent fate, they decide to save their son, placing him in a rocket programmed to travel across the universe to be safe on the distant, alien planet Earth. Upon making this difficult decision, the loving couple knew their son would grow to never know the embrace and love of his birth parents, or, possibly, that they even existed. However, this is not where the story ends. This is where the story begins.

After traveling millions of miles through the hazards of space, the rocket carrying the precious cargo enters Earth's atmosphere and lands in an open field near the Kansas town of Smallville. Serendipitously, a married couple, Jonathan and Martha Kent, unable to have children of their own, find the spacecraft, save the baby, and furtively adopt the black-haired youth to save his life and fill a missing void in their own life. The couple name the boy Clark, love him as if he were their own flesh and blood, and instill in him the foundational lessons of honesty, integrity, truth, justice, and right rather than might in the man who would one day grow to become the superhero Superman.

As a child, Kal-El suffered the trauma of never knowing his birth parents, the beauty and majesty of Krypton, or experience his culture firsthand. However, as a young boy, Clark was also privileged in ways others in similar circumstances may not have been. He did not grow up knowing of Krypton, but he was privileged to have been raised by two loving parents who kept him safe and nurtured his gifts rather than exploit them. This is not to say Clark did not have difficulties throughout his life. Rather, he was offered opportunities for post-traumatic growth following the instances of trauma. Similar to Clark, I suffered trauma as a child but was also privileged in more ways than one.

Throughout our society, privilege has become a dirty word that is synonymous with rich, pampered, and racist. If an individual is called privileged, it is implied that they have been spoiled, have never known hardship, and have it better than most others. While this may be true for some, this is not how I have come to view the word, and it is not how I intend for it to be inferred here. Rather, in my mind, privilege is not synonymous with pampered. Instead, I believe privilege means blessed with opportunity. Individuals who have a privilege have something that benefits their well-being in specific circumstances. It is true, some individuals have more privilege than others, but it does not mean that as a black man I did not and do not enjoy certain privileges in my life. The privileges I have been blessed to have had are not money, or opportunities to gain economic advantages throughout life, but, rather, opportunities to survive, grow, and help others along their journey.

It is true that I suffered childhood sexual abuse from age eight to ten at the hands of my older sister, the domestic abuse of my parents ripped the family apart, and I did not have a home I could call my own during my final two years of high school. All of these factors contributed to my feelings of depression, anxiety, sadness, perfectionism, and workaholism as an adult. However, although the trauma of my childhood had an impact on my mental and physical health then and now, I can recognize that I did have privileges that others may not have had as a person of color in America.

While my father may have been a far cry from father of the year, he was present. The lessons he taught about what it means to be a good man rather than a real man were few and far between, but they were occasional. As a young boy, I also had the privilege of coming home most nights to a two-person household when some of my peers, who were just as black and just as smart as myself, came home to a single parent, grandparent, uncle, aunt, or no parent. Although my father was flawed, and my parents were not the ideal example of a model marriage, they were an example that I had an opportunity to contrast against shows such as *Full House* and

Family Matters. 3027 N. Wilson Dr. eventually became a broken home, but there was laughter, love, and fond memories that I still hold dear as an adult.

Unlike some, I also had the privilege of coming home to a house with furniture, electricity, running water, a kitchen, groceries, clothes, dinner each night, and a bed that was my own. We had cable, a telephone, a washer, dryer, and two cars. Our home may not have always been the most stable, but it was clean, comfortable, and free of drugs. It was a privilege I did not appreciate until it was taken away.

Finally, I had the privilege of receiving a good education from teachers who cared and knew their curriculum. It was public education that taught me the value of reading, friends, socialization, hard work, pride, and perseverance. Without the teachers and coaches of District 150, I would never have received the extensive scholarship package from Bowling Green State University, meet my wife, and become the man I am today. As a public educator myself, I now know quality education in a safe environment is not a guaranteed option for all people of color in this country.

While these privileges may appear unimportant to some, they were vital to my survival. In the same way that Jonathan and Martha Kent provided the foundation for the man Clark would mature into and the hero he would become, my family, home, and schools laid the foundation that allowed me to persevere in the hard times. Life is hard, but survival also means having the humility to count your blessings, no matter how small. It's the mark of a hero. It's the mark of a survivor. It's the mark of an overcomer.

PART FOUR:
CONQUERING THE FACADE

"Remember, son, follow truth, seek justice, and stand with your family who loves you, even when they're not perfect."

Clark Kent—*Superman #45* (2018), "Truth, Justice, Family"

Although association (merging) of a fragmented facade is the goal of this guide, the task of healing and recovery from childhood sexual trauma can often appear difficult if not impossible. The path toward healing can sometimes seem too confusing and disjointed. Male survivors do not know how to begin to properly heal from childhood sexual abuse, let alone recognize a possible path leading toward a finish line. The difficulty of this task can be demonstrated in the evolution and dissociation of the Big Blue Boy Scout himself. Fortunately, the Man of Steel also offers a solution for the daunting task of ending a facade to cope with the trauma of childhood sexual abuse.

Prior to *Crisis on Infinite Earths,* the DC universe had become too large with too many storylines and plot holes throughout the multiverse, creating a universe that had become too fragmented with too many inconsistencies. To remedy the fragmentation of the DC universe, *Crisis on Infinite Earths* destroyed all Earths in the multiverse except one (New Earth). DC events such as *Final Crisis* and *Flashpoint* attempted (but failed) to create consistency throughout the DC universe with the rebirth of characters in the form of the New 52, making a comprehensive Superman storyline almost impossible. The inconsistency only continued into the 1990s when Superman was killed by the villain Doomsday in *The Death of Superman.* When Superman returned, the Big Blue Boy Scout was not the same optimistic beacon of hope as he had been in the 1940s. The superhero had died and been reincarnated so many times in so many alternate plots by so many different writers, Superman was so inconsistent throughout DC's *Superman, Action Comics,* and *Justice League* that he seemed a shell of his former self. Hope of consistency did not arrive until the publication of the major DC event, *Convergence* (2015).

In *Convergence,* Clark Kent, Lois Lane, and their son, Jonathan Kent, are displaced following the destruction of their universe by the villain, Anti-Monitor. They are placed on an Earth in which a Superman, Lois Lane, and Justice League already exist in the form of the New 52. Afterward, in *Superman: Lois and Clark* (2016), Clark and Lois make the decision to go underground and change their last name from Kent to White. Clark grows a beard, leaves the reporting to Lois, becomes a farmer, performs heroic deeds when able to go undetected, and establishes the family of choice he always wished he could but couldn't because of his obligations as Superman.

It is in *Superman: Lois and Clark* that the Clark Kent, Superman, and Kal-El facades begin to fade from existence in a healthy manner. The dissociated identities of Superman, Clark, and Kal-El begin to associate into a complete individual as he reveals his secret to Lois, becoming a loving and open husband and father. The complete association of the different facades of Superman does not take place until the DC Rebirth event in 2016 when all DC characters are rebooted (again) and Clark Kent/White replaces the Superman of New 52 (who dies of kryptonite poisoning). Superman does not truly become the Man of Steel until he makes the choice to remember his forgotten past, associate all the identities and facades he assumed over the eighty years of his existence, and become stronger than he ever imagined possible when he reveals the truth of who he is to the individuals he holds dear.

Association Makes You Stronger

Throughout all comics referenced throughout this guide in which Superman conquers his need for separate identities in the form of a facade, death is a prerequisite. For example, in *Whatever Happened to the Man of Tomorrow*, he enters a room of gold kryptonite to destroy his superhuman abilities. In Alan Moore's *The Jungle Line*, the bloodmorel would have destroyed the hero from the inside out if not for the help of Swamp Thing. Each of these stories teaches the false lesson that something (or some identity) must die to conquer the need to hide behind the false identity of a facade. These comics also teach the false lesson to readers that in order to grow strong, you must first become weak and lose a portion of who you are in order to become stable. These lessons are not accurate when explaining the process of conquering the need to cope with trauma through the use of a facade.

When male survivors make the decision to heal and conquer a dependence on the creation of false identities created by facades, it does not require killing a piece of themselves or becoming weaker to fit in. True healing creates growth, making the survivor stronger than before in the same way Superman becomes stronger after associating his separate identities and choosing to remember the past rather than forget it ever existed in *Superman Rebirth* when Mr. Mxyzptlk assumes the identity of Clark Kent.

Given enough time, survivors who make the conscious decision to not heal often struggle internally with themselves regarding the truth of their past. Rather than face reality, the survivor pushes the trauma away, denies its existence, and attempts to move forward. Unfortunately, moving forward is not an option until the past is remembered and honored. Mxyzptlk and Superman prove this to be true when Jonathan Kent (Superboy) is kidnapped and erased from the memories of his parents, Clark and Lois, in *Superman Reborn* (2016).

Mr. Mxyzptlk is a fifth-dimensional, magical trickster. To him, everything is a game, and people are pieces capable of being manipulated however he sees fit. When Lois and Superman play Mxyzptlk's game to retrieve their son, he changes the rules, forcing the two to lose their memory in the process. Memories not only of Jonathan, but of their relationship together, their marriage to one another, and the family they built with Jonathan. Mxyzptlk's game not only alters the memories of Superman and Lois, but their physical appearance as well when both characters revert back to their New 52 selves. They forget who they are, believing Jonathan is lying when they are reunited.

Mxyzptlk is finally defeated, and reality is corrected when Lois and Superman are merged with their New 52 counterparts, intertwining the identities of the characters and their histories into something new and more powerful. Superman and Lois are not simply pieces that have been put back together. Instead, they have become something new and more powerful. This is what it means to heal from childhood sexual abuse and conquer the need to live a life behind the guise of a facade. Conquering the facade does not mean reverting back to who you were in the past before the abuse occurred. That person no longer exists. It means associating the different identities into something new, better, and more powerful in the same way Jonathan helped merge the old and present selves of Superman and Lois into something new and more stable than either was before. The only way conquering the need to live a false life behind a facade is by saving your Superboy.

Chapter Thirteen: Creating Supermen

"I'm so proud of my heritage. Both from Krypton and Earth. And when I show up as Superman, I want to show up representing both parts of me at the same time."

Superman—*Superman #18* (2019), "Truth"

In 1998, the Center for Disease Control and Kaiser Health Plan's Department of Prevention Medicine conducted an experiment called the Adverse Childhood Experiences (ACE) Study. The ACE study involved the cooperation of over 17,000 middle-aged, middle-class Americans who agreed to help researchers study nine categories of childhood abuse and household dysfunction:

- Recurrent physical abuse
- Recurrent emotional abuse
- Contact sexual abuse
- An alcohol and / or drug abuser in the household
- An incarcerated household member
- A household member who is chronically depressed, mentally ill, institutionalized, or suicidal
- Mother is treated violently
- One or no parents
- Emotional or physical neglect

The study found that as the number of ACEs increased, the risk for health problems increased as well. Health problems such as:

- Alcoholism and alcohol abuse
- Chronic obstructive pulmonary disease (COPD)

- Depression
- Fetal death
- Health-related quality of life
- Illicit drug use
- Ischemic heart disease (IHD)
- Liver disease
- Risk for intimate partner violence
- Multiple sexual partners
- Sexually transmitted diseases (STDs)
- Smoking
- Suicide attempts
- Unintended pregnancies
- Early initiation of smoking
- Early initiation of sexual activity
- Adolescent pregnancy

These health concerns reveal that ACEs have a strong impact on adolescent health, substance abuse, sexual behavior, the risk of revictimization, and stability of relationships. It also means that the higher the ACE score, the greater risk of heart disease, liver disease, HIV, STDs, and other maladies. Individuals with six or more ACEs that were compared to individuals with one or no ACEs were found to have a reduced lifespan of twenty years.

Since the initial study performed in 1998, research has continued to expand to include individuals of different cultural and racial backgrounds across all fifty states. Surveys were distributed to collect data pertaining to ACEs in 2003, 2007, and 2011/12. In 2016, the National Survey of Children's Health (NSCH) continued the ACE study with surveys mailed to a parent or guardian with at least one child, asking a series of yes-or-no questions. Although the questions in this cycle of the survey still remained limited to no more than ten, they were slightly redesigned to include over 50,212 participants. This study found remarkably similar and yet startling different results.

- Economic hardship and divorce or separation of a parent or guardian are the most common ACEs reported nationally and in all states.

- Just under half (45 percent) of children in the United States have experienced at least one ACE.

- One in ten children nationally has experienced three or more ACEs, placing them in high risk. In five states as many as one in seven children had experienced three or more ACEs.

- Children of different races and ethnicities do not experience ACEs equally. Nationally, 61 percent of black non-Hispanic children and 51 percent of Hispanic children have experienced at least one ACE, compared with 40 percent of white non-Hispanic children and only 23 percent of Asian non-Hispanic children. In every division, the prevalence of ACEs is lowest among Asian non-Hispanic children and, in most divisions, is highest among black non-Hispanic children.

This cycle of the study found that not only have ACEs become more prevalent throughout our society, but ACEs are not even shared by children in every state or of every race. ACEs can create toxic levels of stress, fear, terror, and helplessness that can interrupt mental and physical development, creating cognitive distortions and an altered view of the world and of themselves.

As a male survivor of childhood sexual abuse, you may qualify as having many ACEs. Unfortunately, this means your life is more at risk than those who come from stable households with one or no ACEs. The results of this study are extremely troubling and may make you feel as if there is no way toward recovery once childhood trauma, such as childhood sexual abuse, has occurred. This data may make you believe that there is no way to conquer your hypervigilance due to your abuse, and the facades of your Superman have no choice but to continue to not only live, but thrive.

Fortunately, this is not true. The 2016 cycle of the ACE study found that there are ways to prevent or lessen the negative effects of chronic and toxic stress created by ACEs.

Individuals who have a strong understanding of their emotions and work to develop their interpersonal skills were able to lessen the effects of ACEs on their mind and body. The study also found that having a positive, supportive relationship with one or more adults is one of the most important keys to buffering the effects of ACEs. This relationship does not have to be with parents, but it does have to be with an adult who cares about and supports them. This helps to prove that the key to fighting the effects of complex trauma is relationship building. As a male survivor of childhood sexual abuse, attempting to conquer the need for facades includes the need to be, show, and share intimacy as mentors to young men and boys in your care, in your life, and throughout your community. Saving your Superboy includes being a mentor and role model to end the cycle of sexual abuse/assault, but also learning to forgive your inner child.

Fathers Create the Facades of Supermen

The relationships that fathers and father figures build with their sons help determine the man the sons will become. Fatherly actions and words lead boys and young men to reflect on the lessons they are taught and pass them back onto the world in the form of their actions, thoughts, and behaviors. An example of this is in the relationship Superman has with his human father Jonathan Kent and his Kryptonian father Jor-El, without which Superman would have never come to exist.

In *Superman #53* "The Origin of Superman" (1948), Jonathan Kent lays on his deathbed as his son, Clark, sits by his side. In his last few moments of life, he tells Clark:

No man on Earth has the amazing powers you have. You can use them to become a powerful force for good . . . There are evil men in this world. Criminals and outlaws who prey on decent folk! You must fight them in cooperation with the law! To fight those criminals best, you must hide your true identity! They must never know Clark Kent is a super-man. Remember, because that's what you are . . . a Superman!

In this moment, the Clark Kent and Superman facades are born. Rather than remain Clark Kent, a farm boy from Smallville, Kansas, with superhuman abilities, he is told to take on the identity of Superman and the alter ego of Clark Kent to fight crime and bring justice to the world. Throughout Superman's existence, Jonathan has always influenced the way Clark views himself, the world, and his values, but also, at times, causes him to question the truth of his identity.

Like Jonathan Kent, many fathers and other male role models tell boys and young men to blindly follow the boy code by remaining stoic, seemingly in control, and a real man who doesn't put up with "sissy stuff." These fathers and role models sometimes perpetuate these lessons through their words, but many times they perpetuate the false expectations of manhood through their actions and behaviors that boys mimic in an attempt to be accepted. This code tells boys and young men that they cannot be sexually abused or assaulted. It also tells boys and young men that they should always want (and be searching for) sex, hide their feelings, and take what they want when it is not given freely. It creates the facade of Superman that seeks to achieve perfectionism by sacrificing the Superboy in the form of their son and their inner child. This is not only true for Jonathan Kent and the Superman facade, but for the Jor-El and the Kal-El facade as well.

In the same way Jonathan Kent had a hand in creating Clark's Superman facade, Jor-El contributed to the creation of the Kal-El facade. As a boy, Clark does not get the opportunity to meet his biological father, Jor-El. Instead, he is given words of advice and tidbits of information from a holographic image projected from the rocket Clark used to arrive on Earth. In *Superman: Secret Origin*, Jor-El tells his son:

> You will be protected on this new world by the abilities its environment will provide you. You will be free to move among the people of Earth. But never forget, although you look like one of them, you are not one of them.

Jor-El reiterates this to Superman as an adult in the Fortress of Solitude when he tells Kal-El:

> You must remember you were sent here because you look like one of them, but you are not one of them. Our culture survives with you. And the hope we had for our future can be shared with the people on Earth by you, the last son of Krypton.

Jor-El makes his son believe he will always be alone and separate from the people he cares about.

These examples demonstrate how fathers and other male role models have an impact on males and their development into "real men" or "good men," depending on the relationships they build with one another. Choosing to heal from the trauma of childhood sexual abuse associates the facades into a complete individual capable of guiding and mentoring other boys and young men in a way that ends the cycle of perpetuating the good-guy code, the Superman code, and the boy code. On the other hand, choosing to continue to cope with the trauma of childhood sexual abuse with the facade of Clark Kent, Superman, or Kal-El helps to ensure boys and young men continue to mask their emotions and live a life of depression, anxiety, and fear. The only solution to ending the cycle of sexual assault of both men and women is by choosing to heal. It is the only way to save your Superboy.

Chapter Fourteen: Conquering Your Superman

"Thank you, Ma and Pa. Since we've had Jon, I think I understand the things you tried to teach me a little bit better. Together as a family we're seeing to it that we pass those values on to the next generation."

Clark Kent—*Superman #45* (2018), "Truth, Justice, Family"

The #MeToo movement has begun to bring the impact of sexual assault and rape from the shadows of our society into the harsh light of reality. Startling statistics have been revealed about the sexual abuse and assault of both men and women. For example, in 2019, the *Journal of the American Medical Association* published a report that revealed over 3.3 million women's first sexual experience was rape. That is one in sixteen women stating that their first act of sexual intercourse was forced or coerced, with many stating it occurred as early as fifteen. Sexual abuse and assault has not only increased for girls and women, but children too.

JAMA Pediatrics published a report in 2019 that explained how the number of adolescents admitted to the emergency room for injuries related to sexual assault increased from 2,280 in 2010 to 5,058 in 2016. While these statistics are alarming, the Center for Disease Control and Prevention published a report equally as troubling that explains how in 2019 the suicide rate among young Americans aged ten to twenty-four rose by 56 percent between 2007 and 2017. Also startling is that 79 percent of all suicide deaths are men.

Sexual assault and abuse impact society in many negative ways. Men and women who are sexually abused as children sometimes do not make the choice to heal from the trauma of their past, resulting in anxiety, depression, and living life behind a facade. While the sexual assault and abuse is not the fault of the victim, they have the responsibility to heal. Not doing so leads to hatred that is toxic to themselves and others.

The words and actions of father figures and role models shape the way boys view themselves and their actions. The ACE study helps to demonstrate how children who have suffered C-PTSD need positive role models to reverse the effects on the mind and body caused by adverse childhood experiences. Without positive male role models, male survivors can be manipulated into creating a facade that abides by the false misconceptions of the good-guy code, hero code, and boy code, eventually transforming the thoughts and actions of the survivor into those of a victim.

In the same way that there is a difference between a hero and a villain, there is also a difference between a victim and a survivor. The actions of Superboy-Prime in the graphic novel *Infinite Crisis* helps to demonstrate how survivors and victims may be different from the other, but also how quickly a survivor's actions and thoughts can transform into those of a victim.

Failing Your Superboy

In the graphic novel *Crisis on Infinite Earths*, the multiverse is destroyed and only one Earth exists. The heroes of the other worlds either vanish from existence or are integrated into the timeline of the New Earth. The characters who are a part of the multiverse who survive and exist in a pocket dimension looking over Earth are Alexander Luthor, Superboy-Prime, and Superman and Lois Lane of Earth-Two. From this pocket dimension, they watch the actions of the heroes of Earth and live in a state of paradise.

Later, in *Infinite Crisis* and following the actions of *Crisis on Infinite Earths*, the paradise created by Alexander Luthor's pocket dimension comes to an end when these four individuals attempt to destroy New-Earth and recreate the multiverse. Superman and Superboy-Prime are convinced by Luthor that New-Earth is corrupt, flawed, and in need of true heroes (like themselves) capable of fixing the mistake made when the multiverse was destroyed. After escaping the pocket dimension, Superboy-Prime fights and eventually kills Connor (along with a few other characters), the Superboy of New-Earth. Superboy-Prime does this because he is brainwashed by Luthor to believe he is the "real" Superboy while Connor is a "fake" and imperfect clone of Superman.

Throughout Superboy-Prime and Connor's fight, readers view how misguided actions and confused thoughts can quickly lead a hero down the path of becoming a villain. Believing he is the hero, Superboy-Prime questions why the characters he view as heroes like himself are fighting to defend Connor, whom he views as fake and imperfect. He says, "What are you doing? I'm not a bad guy!" as the Teen Titans fight to restrain him. Later, he becomes so angry he decapitates a hero. Afterward, with tears in his eyes, he looks at the blood on his hands and says, "Oh no! I didn't mean to do that . . . Please! I said I didn't mean to!" Unfortunately, he becomes so enraged at his actions that he kills multiple other heroes, blaming his actions on others when he says, "Why are you making me? Why?! You're ruining everything! You're ruining me! You're making me like you!" As Flash pushes Superboy into the Speed Force to keep him from killing anyone else, he screams, "You can't get rid of me! When I grow up I'm going to be Superman! Don't any of you understand?! I'm going to be Superman!"

With these words, it proves Superboy-Prime was right. He was going to grow up to be Superman. He already was Superman. He lived life behind a facade of what it meant to be "real," transforming his actions from those of a hero into those of a villain. Superboy-Prime's transformation is what takes place externally and internally when male survivors do not develop positive relationships to combat the effects of adverse childhood experiences. Survivors of childhood sexual abuse who do not make the choice to heal have the potential to begin viewing their actions as those of a victim by refusing to forgive their inner child of a crime they blame themselves for being unable to prevent. These thoughts cause male survivors to project the same rage as Superboy-Prime outward toward others in the form of abuse and inward toward themselves in the form of self-harm and suicide. The only way to save your Superboy is through the development of positive relationships and making the choice to heal the trauma caused by childhood sexual abuse.

The unfortunate result of the trauma of childhood sexual abuse for male survivors is that they never feel as though they are worthy of being called men due to the perpetuated belief that men and boys cannot be sexually abused or assaulted. It is for this reason they believe sexual abuse makes them less of a man. A male survivor's desire to be seen as and to feel "real" can fill them with the same rage as Superboy-Prime in *Infinite Crisis*. However, developing positive relationships and expressing emotions in a healthy way can make male survivors feel as though they have someone fighting on their side in the same manner as Superboy (Jonathan Kent) in *Superman: Rebirth (2016)*. It can guide male survivors toward believing they are enough regardless of their past trauma and help replace the need to be seen as a real man with the desire to be a good man.

Saving Your Superboy

In *Superman #2-7* (2016), "The Son of Superman: Part 1-6" (2016), Superman battles the villain, Eradicator for the life of his son, Jonathan, who is the son of Clark and Lois. In these first few comics of *Superman*, readers are introduced to the Eradicator. This villain possesses the souls of dead Kryptonians in his body, seeking to cleanse Jonathan of his humanity to make him a pure Kryptonian like Superman. He tells Superman while in the Fortress of Solitude:

For Krypton to truly be reborn in all its glory, our species needs to propagate. But to preserve the purity of the race the Kryptonian genome needs to be uncorrupted. We shall start with your offspring and find a way to bolster his Kryptonian genome to subsume his human one.

Rather than continue to live behind a Kal-El facade, Superman fights for his son and the belief that Jon is not less but more because of his humanity. When the Eradicator tells Superman:

You defy your heritage. Your blood is our blood. Our blood is your blood. That is why you do not fight with full force. You are fearful of harming the Kryptonians within us. We are your home. Your home is you . . . How far will you plunge the future of El into Darkness?! How long will you suppress their legacy in the offspring of a foreign world?!

Superman only response is, "This is my home—my family—and delusional soul-sucking abominations won't lecture me on how to keep my boy safe!" These are the words boys who have been sexually abused desperately wish to hear following their sexual assault. Male survivors want to know they are loved and wanted regardless of whether or not they live up to society's standards of what it means to be a real man.

As an adult male survivor of childhood sexual abuse, choosing to heal means forgiving, nurturing, and comforting your inner Superboy, who believes the sexual assault was his fault. It means fighting for your inner Superboy to drop the good-guy, people-pleasing facade of Clark Kent, and to set realistic boundaries that ensure the preservation of your mental health. It means allowing your inner Superboy the opportunity to alter their hero code, drop the Superman facade, and know that sometimes it is okay to not be okay. Finally, it means allowing your inner Superboy to break the boy code, shatter the Kal-El facade, and have the courage to transform into someone stronger and better than you ever believed possible.

Afterward, you pass these lessons onto your own Superboy to reverse the effects of adverse childhood experiences and end the cycle of sexual abuse and assault for men and women by replacing real men with good men. Clark teaches these lessons to Jonathan in *Superman #45* (2018), "Truth, Justice, Family." While standing in the center of their farm, Clark tells Jonathan:

> Son, you're getting big enough to learn that sometimes life isn't fair. Things change. We always hope for the best, but never forget—the world doesn't owe you a thing . . . It's a hard truth that far too many men forget, but the point is that only you can choose who to be when things don't go your way. That's the difference between someone who helps others and someone who helps themselves.

The sexual abuse was not your fault, but it is your responsibility to heal. Helping others and passing on what you have learned is the final step on your journey to recovery. It is the only way to break the cycle of sexual abuse and become more than "super." We get to be ourselves.

Chapter Fifteen: Saving My Superboy (Autobiographical)

"It's a hard truth that far too many forget, but the point is that only you can choose who to be when things don't go your way. That's the difference between someone who helps others and someone who helps themselves."

Clark Kent—*Superman #45* (2018), "Truth, Justice, Family"

It's a hardcover *Goosebumps* notebook that was bought from Borders Bookstore sometime in the late 1990s. Although I enjoyed watching *Goosebumps,* the television show, the horror stories written by R. L. Stine never held my attention in the same way as my peers. It's for this reason I'm not exactly sure why I bought the notebook and decided to make it the journal in which I wrote all my thoughts throughout most of middle and high school. Perhaps it was because the pages were empty of words and I thought it would be cool to write my own stories, but there's no way to know for certain since the first pages have been ripped from the spine. I guess the writing was not to my liking.

Although I did not enjoy reading *Goosebumps,* I was obsessed with Dragon Ball Z. At this same time, I also became obsessed with learning to draw (which I never mastered). That's why the outside cover of the once-green slime-colored notebook is now filled with poorly traced and printed pictures of Goku going Super Saiyan taped to the front and back cover.

Inside the notebook, many of the pages have poorly written sentences and paragraphs explaining a young black boy's desperate attempt to find love and overdramatically details the injustices of life forced on a preteen. Some have dates, most are poorly written, and others offer an insight into a young man's desperate need for someone to communicate about depression, anxiety, and basic human emotions. The boy who wrote those words has not vanished from existence, but he has changed. For a long time he was locked away and shamed into silence. To allow my inner child an opportunity to regain his voice and grow, I came to realize he needed to be forgiven for past traumas he had little control in dictating.

Using my old journal, I revisit the boy of my past, listen to what he has to say, acknowledge his feelings, and forgive him for traumatic moments he had no control over. The words of my past act as my time machine in an attempt to save my inner Superboy.

1/27/01

My whole life is a joke. I'm so different from everyone else. Everyone is so good at everything, and then look at me. Maybe one day I'll amount to something worthwhile, but maybe not. I'm beginning to have doubts about my dream. I may not make it to become the first black president. I think I'll grow up to become another face in the crowd and be forgotten about when I die. My feelings may change one day, but for right now this is the way I feel.

Later Days,

Kenny

Kenny,

First, let me tell you that your life is not a joke. It never was a joke. It will never be a joke. Everyone has good and bad days, but all lives have a purpose, even if it doesn't seem that they do. I know you feel like you're living life without a safety net, filled with so much fear about what the next day, week, month, and years will hold, but you have some good days ahead. Unfortunately, you won't become the first black president (Barack will beat you to the punch), but you will witness the birth of your two lovely daughters, Mirus and Amare; you'll go through the torment of losing your son, Casus, and the feeling of hopelessness at being unable to prevent his death; you'll write books and stories with the ability to whisk strangers away to the depths of your imagination, the corners of your nightmares, and the complex beauty of understanding the thoughts and feelings needed to heal from traumas of the past. You're an amazing young man and you're going to eventually grow up to be a good man, teacher, dad, and husband.

From the future,

Kenny

5/29/01

I don't know how to start. Well, I can mark this as the day I found out I was black. You're probably wondering what I mean, but that's just what I said. I was at play rehearsal for Bye, Bye Birdie *and it hit me. I was the only black person. I started to think of why I didn't have a girlfriend and why some of the people there liked the other leads. It was because they were the same race as them. People are attracted to people that they hang around the most. The race of people that are in their surroundings most of the time. That's why I was attracted to white people that I hung out with, had about the same personality, and were my friends. So, I'm just sort of a freak. I have a great personality, polite, I don't look bad, but I'm black. How many black people do you know that are like me? Not many. I'm accepted by whites, but there will always be that discomfort that will never go away. I can only hope that I can find a black girl in college that matches my personality. I know it's not going to happen in high school. If it doesn't happen in college then I will be a single president. Well, gotta go.*

Later days,

Ynnek

Ynnek,

Wow! Freak? Those are some harsh words. Is that something you would have said to another person? Even your worst enemy? Are those the words of a hero or a villain? You have to learn to treat yourself better. It's a lesson that will take years of therapy and consistent practice to begin to comprehend. While you may enjoy being in plays, acting, running, and writing, these activities do not make you a freak. In fact, it makes you courageous for having the fortitude to not follow the crowd and rather do what you enjoy. Skin color has nothing to do with doing what you love. Eventually, you will learn skin color has little to do with love, but a lot to do with having the patience and trust to grow, mature, and raise a family with another person regardless of their skin color or sexual orientation. Be you, young man. Other people will come to depend on you continuing to be you. Stay strong, my little Viking!

Later days from the future,

Kenny

It's the Saturday of the Cross Country Peoria High Invite. I should be running, but I'm going to take two days off. Not because I'm lazy, but because I think I need to take a break. I want to run, but it will probably be best if I let my will to run run through me and simmer a little. Use it as running fuel. It's full right now, but I'm going to let it run over. Oh, yeah, everyone thinks I'm suicidal. Well, on the day of the last meet I wrote Adam a note telling him I got another ride home. The only thing is, I wrote it creatively because I thought they might get a kick out of it. Well, they didn't! They read the note that was in Adam's locker and the Buddies took it seriously and gave it to Coach. So, Coach Poehls calls me to see if I'm okay and says that he sent someone over to Bradley Park to look for me and I shouldn't joke around like that. We got off the phone and the anger from the CC meet had left me and had been replaced with feeling bad for writing the note, so I decided to call Adam and apologize for the note, but he wasn't there yet. So, after about two minutes of getting off the phone with Adam's brother, I hear someone knock on my window from the kitchen. Of course, it's Adam because he's the only one that knocks on my window. So, when I head out, I'm very surprised to see Pat, Brian, and Adam. That made me feel really awful. They were relieved when they found out it was a joke, then they beat me up about three times. Then, ten minutes later, Coach stops by to make sure I'm okay. Eventually, they all left and I felt awful. Coach called my mom the next day at work, but I had already told her. The funny thing is though, my mom was thinking the same thing. Pretty weird. Coach advised my mom to get me counseling. My mom talked to me then my dad talked to me. So now everyone is watching me so I have to keep on a fake person act to keep them off my back. Oh well. It was a joke and that's all, whether they believe it or not. God will help!

Later Days,

Kenny

Kenny,

I remember that day. I remember writing the letter, leaving it in Adam's locker and thinking it was creative. Unfortunately, I also remember lying when I said it was a joke. I did want to kill myself. Maybe not on that day in that way, but I did want to die. I wanted to find some way to relieve the pressure of living in constant fear and the sense of being a perpetual failure. You will remember these feelings and this letter each time a student shares a story of struggling to sleep because of his parents arguing, not having a safe place to sleep because their family is homeless, or asking for a granola bar because they did not eat breakfast that morning for one reason or another. Somedays, remembering how you felt while writing that letter and wishing it would come true is the only reason you decide to keep showing up to work. Because, like you, they will lie to others and themselves about how they truly feel and how they want the pain to stop. Keep helping. Keep going. You're doing good. You're doing your best.

From the future,

Kenny

11/22/01

I'm a little bored and lonely and decided to write before I take a shower. Well, it's Thanksgiving! Thanksgiving . . . I just now thought about actually giving thanks. Most people don't really remember to give thanks on Thanksgiving. Here are my thanks. Dear Lord, I am thankful to be alive today. To experience the world and all of the knowledge and wonder. I give thanks for my family and my health. I am thankful to have friends and family that care about me. I'm thankful to be in my right state of mind. I'm thankful for all of the gifts that God has blessed me with. I am thankful for my health. I'm thankful for all of the lessons that the Lord has put me through. But most of all, I am thankful to be thankful.

Happy Thanksgiving.

Kenny Rogers Jr.

Kenny,

Never stop being thankful and forgiving of yourself and others while continuing to hold them accountable.

Love,

Kenny

When I Heard the Learn'd Astronomer

By Walt Whitman

When I heard the learn'd astronomer.

When the proofs, the figures, were ranged in columns before me

When I was shown the charts and diagrams, to add, divide and measure them

When I sitting heard the astronomer where he lectured with much applause in the lecture-room.

How soon unaccountable I became tired and sick,

Till rising and gliding out I wander'd off by myself

In the mystical moist night-air, and from time to time,

Look'd up in perfect silence at the stars.

Kenny,

Your imagination will someday save you from insanity. Hear the "learn'd" people of the world, heed their lessons, but retain the wonder, awe, and humility from the vastness of the heavens above. Remember this as well:

"If"

By Rudyard Kipling

If you can keep your head when all about you

Are losing theirs and blaming it on you,

If you can trust yourself when all men doubt you,

But make allowance for their doubting too;

If you can wait and not be tired by waiting,

Or being lied about, don't deal in lies,

Or being hated, don't give way to hating,

And yet don't look too good, nor talk too wise:

If you can dream—and not make dreams your master;

If you can think—and not make thoughts your aim;

If you can meet with Triumph and Disaster

And treat those two imposters just the same;

If you can bear to hear the truth you've spoken

Twisted by knaves to make a trap for fools,

Or watch the things you give life to, broken,

And stoop and build 'em up with worn-out tools

If you can make one heap of all your winnings,

And risk it on one turn of pitch-and-toss,

And lose, and start again at your beginnings

And never breathe a word about your loss;

If you can force your heart and nerve and sinew

To serve your turn long after they are gone,

And so hold on when there is nothing in you

Except the will which says to them: 'Hold on!'

If you can talk with crowds and keep your virtue,

Or walk with Kings—nor lose common touch,

If neither foes nor loving friends can hurt you,

If all men count with you, but none too much;

If you can fill the unforgiving minute

With sixty seconds' worth of distance run,

Yours is the Earth and everything that's in it,

And—which is more—you'll be a Man, my son!

3/13/02

I've decided to write before I pack this book away with all the others. I've been meaning to write a lot, but I never have my journal.

Here it is. Love. What is this thing that people call love? I don't think it's what everyone says it is. I think that it's a disease. A disease that feeds on everyone that catches it. When someone gets it, they think that it's good and feels good. How wrong they are. That love, that happiness, that warm tingling feeling that they say they have is actually just the opposite. The disease sucks the person in so they can't get out by making them believe it's good. When in all actuality it is taking away their happiness. It sucks the happiness out of a person. Slow at first and then faster. Soon, all that's left is a mean bitter person. I know it's true because I've seen it happen with my parents. And I see it happening with my sister and brother. This love that everyone wants is just a wolf in sheep's clothing. But I have found the culprit and I will not be fooled! Other idiots can have their love while I remain strong. I've seen what it did to my parents and that will not happen to me. Fuck love and everything about it. It's a hollow and empty word that leaves you that way. And that is not how I want to end up. Day of departure from the only home I've ever known.

Kenny

Kenny,

This was a big day. It was a day that will define a large part of your life. You lost your home. It was difficult to endure, and because of this moment you became afraid that everything could be taken away no matter how hard you tried to hold it tight, but don't let the actions of others turn your heart to stone. Love is important and needed to grow. The foreclosure of 3027 N. Wilson Dr. was not your fault. These were actions you could not control. What you experienced as a child was not love. Learn and teach love and patience to those around you. It will come back to you threefold. Don't give up on love because it hasn't given up on you.

Later days,

Kenny

What the fuck have I been doing for the past two years? Do I have any idea who I am or what I've done? What have I done that has been any consequence since I have been in school? Nothing! I've read. I am an amazing person and I've been afraid of life for two years. Ever since graduation the world has seemed too big with too many options. Kenny was quiet yet outgoing. He spent hours alone in his room doing homework, memorizing scripts, reading books. Hours running through the city, participating in school activities, laughing and joking with friends. But, Kenny was just a child then. Life had not begun until things got too real for him. The moving from one house to the next and getting more miserable by the day. He went through the motions because that is what he always did. He forgot why he did all those things. He loved the sense of accomplishment he got once he completed a task. It was not easy, and that is what made it worthwhile. The fact that he had to work for it. But things changed and he forgot all of this. When the motions finally stopped he realized he had lost himself somewhere along the way, but where? So, he searched. Hiding and afraid to go out and be adventurous again. As he did this, he forgot. He became like everyone else, but still thought of himself as that boy from the past that was lost. Not too many people saw this outstanding person in him, because he didn't really see it in himself. He was average, but not quite. Superman had lost his powers, but he was still a hero. Eventually, Kenny completely forgot who he used to be and believed the person he was now was the person he had always been. Until one day, he remembered. He remembered he was searching for something when he saw a glimpse of his old life. I saw awards for outstanding athlete, a letter of appreciation from fraternities for winning their contests and scholarships, award letters for Who's Who and National Honor Roll and countless other things. Many people had achieved this status and received these awards, but few carried themselves the way I did. I know that in my face people could see something special. I was a good person who people trusted and looked up to. And I forgot that. I've seen a lot and the world is big and it is frightening, but so has been most of the experiences for the last twenty years of my life. I stepped up to the challenge and passed. Looking forward to the next. I fell once and lost myself, but I'm growing and this is a new Kenny. Improved, but still flawed. But the flaws do not stop me, only give me more fuel to push forward. I am an outstanding person who can and has done outstanding things, but none of it came easy. I believed for a while that it should be easy, so my outstandingness stopped. Not anymore. Fear, I know you will come, but I will not let that stop me. I am twenty now. It is about time to start becoming the man I was supposed to be. If you want to be a knight, be a knight. If you want to be a man, be a man. No more. I have found myself by taking a look into the past. I know who I once was and who I want to be. I will become that person. I may fall and stumble at times, but with God's help I will see it through. He has helped me through these past 2-4 years more than I will ever know and I love Him for it. No more writing for now, just doing. "Some people rise by sin others fall by virtue." I would rather fall by virtue than rise by sin.

Kenny,

Something really bad happened to you. Actually, multiple really bad things happened to you before the age of eighteen. You were sexually abused, assaulted, and raped by age eight. You witnessed the domestic abuse of your mother and brother. You were homeless by age sixteen. Throughout all of this, you kept going. You never stopped. You never gave up. At the time you believed these moments made you strong, but these moments did not *make* you strong. You were already strong. Your ability to endure with grace and achieve success proves your strength. This does not make you Superman, or a superhero. You're human, and you're allowed to rest. You had some major accomplishments in the past, and you will achieve more accomplishments in the future. There will also be more setbacks, more fear, more love, more tears, more good days, and more bad days, but they are all worth it. Take the past, learn from it, and pass the wisdom on to the others. It's why you're here. It gives you purpose and provides others with the strength needed to rise and meet the challenges of a new day. Success may come in two months, two years, twenty years, or never at all. However, success is not the goal. Rather, the goal is growth. Learning to breathe, endure, rest, replenish, fall, and rise to meet the next challenge. Keep going. Keep stumbling. Keep rising. And soon, success *may* come as well.

FURTHER READING

"I have to leave Smallville. I have to seek out the people and places that *need* somebody who can do the things I can do."

Clark Kent—*Superman: The Man of Steel* (1986)

The comics referenced throughout this guide, along with the books detailing and describing the different forms of therapy used in order to heal, are included below. As mentioned in the introduction, I am not a psychiatrist, therapist, or counselor. Neither am I an expert on all things Superman. With that said, if any material in this book is inaccurate in its information, I sincerely ask your apology. This guide was written in an attempt to help male survivors, like myself, understand the trauma of their sexual abuse in a manner they find familiar, comfortable, and beneficial on their path to recovery. Use this list of sources to buy, read, and give respect to the artists and writers who created the fantastically detailed universe people across the globe have grown to love. Use this list to not only further your reading of comics, but to also acquire more tools to accompany you along your journey of recovery to heal the childhood trauma of sexual abuse.

Sources

Action Comics #242 (1958), "The Super-Duel in Space"

Action Comics #775 (2001), "What's So Funny About Truth, Justice and the American Way?"

Action Comics #900 (2011), "The Incident"

All-Star Superman (2011)

Convergence (2015)

Huck Book One: All-American (2016)

Infinite Crisis (2006)

Injustice: Gods Among Us Year One—The Complete Collection (2016)

Justice (2011)

Kingdom Come (2008)

Luthor (2015)

Superman #2 (2016), "Son of Superman: Part 3"

Superman #2 (2018), "The Unity Saga: Part 2"

Superman #4 (2016), "Son of Superman: Part 4"

Superman #5 (2016), "Son of Superman: Part 5"

Superman #6 (2018), "The Unity Saga: Part 6"

Superman #45 (2018), "Truth, Justice, Family"

Superman #53 (1948), "The Origin of Superman"

Superman #141 (1960), "Superman's Return to Krypton"

Superman #149 (1960), "The Death of Superman"

Superman #247 (1972), "Must There Be a Superman?"

Superman: American Alien (2017)

Superman Annual #11 (1985), "For the Man Who Has Everything"

Superman: Brainiac (2018)

Superman: Earth One (2010)

Superman: For All Seasons (2018)

Superman: Last Son (2008)

Superman: Lois and Clark (2016)

Superman Reborn (2018)

Superman: Red Son (2014)

Superman: Secret Identity—The Deluxe Edition (2015)

Superman: Secret Origin (2018)

Superman: The Final Days of Superman (2016)

Superman: The Man of Steel (1986)

The Body Keeps the Score: Brain, Mind, and Body in the Healing of Trauma (2015) by Bessel Van der Kolk, MD

The Complex PTSD Workbook: A Mind-Body Approach to Regaining Emotional Control and Becoming Whole (2016) by Arielle Schwartz

The Courage to Heal: A Guide for Woman Survivors of Child Sexual Abuse (1992) by Ellen Bass and Laura Davis

The Jungle Line (1985)

The Man of Steel (2018)

The PTSD Workbook (2016)

Trauma and Recovery (1992)

Whatever Happened to the Man of Tomorrow (1986)

GLOSSARY

"You don't need a Superman! What you really need is a super-will to be guardians of your own destiny!"

Superman—*Superman* #247 (1972), "Must There Be a Superman?"

The DC universe is vast in size and characters. Sometimes the amount of information needed to read a comic can pose a challenge for readers. This glossary is meant to help reduce some of those obstacles for readers who may wish to read and learn from this guide, but not know much about Superman, Metropolis, Clark Kent, and the distant world of Krypton. Unfortunately, I am not an expert on all things Superman. Most of what I know I learned while researching this guide. If there are any inaccuracies in my information in this glossary or throughout this guide, I am sorry. The Superman mythos is everchanging, but interesting, beautiful, and filled with hope. Let that hope spread and help throughout your recovery.

B

Batman: The mortal superhero known as "The Dark Knight" whose secret identity is Bruce Wayne.

Black Mercy: A tentacled alien plant that latches onto the chest of its host, building a psychic connection that provides a realistic fantasy while feeding on their life force.

Brainiac: Alien supervillain from the planet Colu, or evolved supercomputer and destroyer of the planet Krypton, seeking to consume knowledge from other alien species before destroying the planet and preserving a single city and its inhabitants in a bottle if the species is considered highly evolved.

C

Christopher Kent: Also known as Lor-Zod, he is the son of Kryptonian villains General Zod and Ursa who was born inside the Phantom Zone and is immune to the Phantom Zone's effects.

Clark Kent: Often described as mild-mannered, Clark Kent is the alter ego of Superman and was raised in Smallville, Kansas, by Jonathan and Martha Kent. As an adult he is a reporter for the Metropolis City newspaper the *Daily Planet.*

D

Daily Planet: Newspaper of Metropolis City at which Clark Kent and Lois Lane are investigative reporters, Perry White is the editor in chief, and Jimmy Olson is the photographer.

Diana Prince: See Wonder Woman.

F

Flash: Superhero with the ability of super speed whose alter ego is forensic scientist Barry Allen.

Fortress of Solitude: Location in the North Pole where Superman adjourns to collect his thoughts and honor his Kryptonian heritage.

G

General Zod: Villain from the planet Krypton with the same super abilities as Superman but seeking to preserve and resurrect the Kryptonian culture by any means necessary.

J

Jimmy Olsen: Photographer and errand boy for the Metropolis City newspaper, the *Daily Planet*. He is considered a close friend of Superman but does not know Clark Kent is Superman.

Joker: Supervillain and archnemesis of Batman who thrives on chaos and is depicted as a clown with a white face, green hair, and a wide grin.

Jonathan Kent: Farmer, husband of Martha Kent, and adopted father of Clark Kent.

Jonathan Kent / White: Also known as Superboy, he is the son of Lois Lane and Clark Kent. He possess the same abilities as Superman.

Jor-El: Father of Kal-El who, moments before the planet Krypton was destroyed, placed his son in a rocket sent to planet Earth to save his life.

K

Kal-El: Kryptonian name of Superman.

Kandor: Capital city of the planet Krypton that was shrunk and bottled by the villain Brainiac before its destruction.

Krypton: Birth planet of the hero Superman that exploded, destroying most of its people and leaving Superman one of the few Kryptonian survivors.

Kryptonite: Radioactive pieces of the planet Krypton which produce different effects on Kryptonians depending on their color, such as green, black, red, gold, and white.

L

Lana Lang: Childhood friend and love interest of Clark Kent from Smallville, Kansas, who is one of the few who know Clark Kent is also Superman.

Lara: Birth mother of Kal-El, who made the decision, along with her husband, Jor-El, to save the life of their only son by placing him in a rocket sent to Earth moments before the planet Krypton's destruction.

Lex Luthor: Archnemesis of Superman who is a genius, devotes his resources toward destroying the Man of Steel, and wants nothing more than to see the hero suffer and die.

Lois Lane: Investigative reporter for the newspaper the *Daily Planet*, wife of Clark Kent, mother of Jonathan Kent (Superboy), and one of the few characters who knows Clark Kent is also Superman.

Lor-Zod: See Christopher Kent.

Lyla Lerrol: Kryptonian actress and love interest of Kal-El when Superman visited Krypton in the past, and in the fantasy created by the alien, symbiotic, and psychic plant, Black Mercy.

M

Martha Kent: Farmer, wife of Jonathan Kent, and adopted mother of Clark Kent.

Metallo: Cyborg supervillain, also known as Sergeant John Corben of the United States Army, who uses his super strength and kryptonite as weapons in an attempt to kill Superman.

Metropolis City: City in which Clark Kent lives, works, and protects as the hero, Superman.

Mr. Mxyzpltk: Fifth-dimensional villain and trickster who uses magic as a weapon in an attempt to defeat Superman.

P

Perry White: Editor in chief of the Metropolis City newspaper the *Daily Planet.*

Pete Ross: Childhood best friend from Smallville, Kansas, that eventually discovers Clark Kent is Superman.

Phantom Zone: Alternate dimension discovered by Jor-El, where the people of the planet Krypton placed its most ruthless criminals rather than sentence them to death.

R

Rogol Zaar: Supervillain from the planet Krypton who is responsible for the destruction of the planet Krypton, the desolation of the bottle city of Kandor, and the attempted genocide of the Kryptonian race.

S

Superman: Superhero born on the planet Krypton, given the name Kal-El, but known by many on Earth as "The Man of Steel," and "The Big Blue Boy Scout," he conceals his super strength, super speed, and ability to fly using the alter ego Clark Kent.

Superboy: See Jonathan White/Kent.

Superboy-Prime: Hero turned villain who survived the Anti-Monitor's attempt to eliminate the multiverse and sought to bring back his Earth with the help of Alexander Luthor.

V

Van-El: Son of Kal-El and Lyla Lerrol in the fantasy dream created during the symbiotic and psychic connection of the Black Mercy and Superman.

W

Wonder Woman: Amazonian princess Diana Prince and superhero who has the super abilities of super strength, flight, and wields a magic lasso endowed with the ability to compel men to the truth.

CPSIA information can be obtained
at www.ICGtesting.com
Printed in the USA
FSHW012341260320
68519FS